Dear Steph°
Congratulations _____
Ireland! May your new
travels be full of sun,
warmth, fun and great
food — yummy, yummy!
Love Minty Pinhead freak!

hotels · villas · restaurants · spas · wineries · galleries · marinas

croatiachic

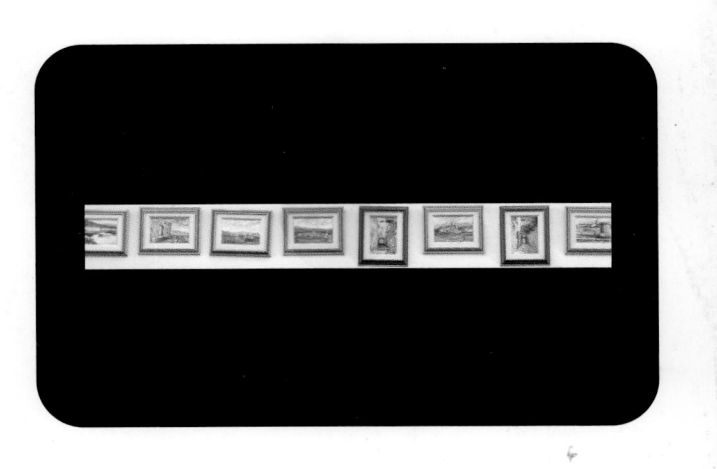

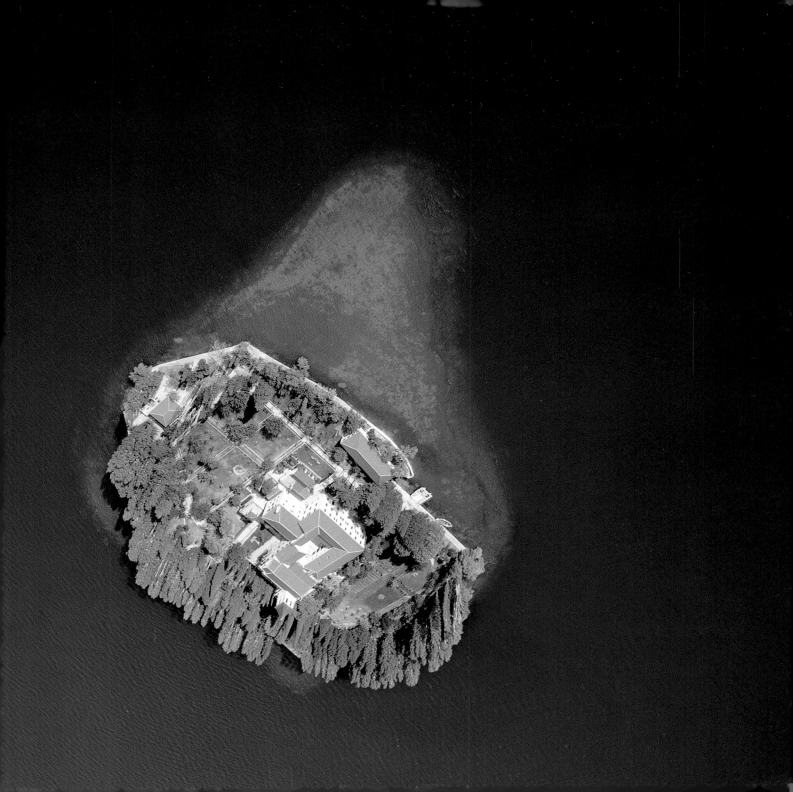

hotels • villas • restaurants • spas • wineries • galleries • marinas

croatiachic

text françoise raymond kuijper • kerry o'neill • richard nichols

·K·U·P·E·R·A·R·D·

acknowledgements

The much-awaited *Croatia Chic* is finally here, profiling the very best the country has to offer, including its hotels, villas, restaurants, spas, wineries, galleries and marinas. This book has come a long way, and thanks are due to all those who have made it possible.

The properties featured in *Croatia Chic* are owed thanks for their cooperation and contributions, without which this book would not exist. The entire team in the Croatian National Tourist Board in Paris have also been invaluable, particularly director Marina Tomas-Billet, whose tireless efforts never cease to amaze, Christine Delort, Ivana Benkotic and Ingrid Poupry, as well as Josip Lozic their colleague in London, all who helped to move this project forward immeasurably.

Not forgotten are Mirjana Resner, head of operational marketing from the Croatian National Tourism Board's head office in Zagreb and Tonci Skyrce, director of the Dubrovnik Tourist Board, both of whom provided countless opportunities and contacts instrumental in this publication. Special mentions go out to Robertina Majstrovic, French regional manager of Croatia Airlines, Marc van Bloemen of Karmendu Apartments in Dubrovnik, and all at Suncani Hvar Hotels—Jean-François Ott and Jacques Bourgeois are due especial thanks—for their continual support.

Françoise Kuijper has produced yet another quality *Chic* book; she and the indefatigable Isabelle du Plessix have been, without exaggeration, indispensable throughout the entirety of this project. The publisher would further like to extend gratitude to all readers who share with us a profound appreciation of the beautiful country of Croatia, and hopes this will be only the beginning of a long and fulfilling relationship with this destination of destinations.

executive editor
melisa teo

editor
candice lim

assistant editor
suzanne wong

designers
nelani jinadasa
norreha sayuti

production manager
sin kam cheong

first published in 2007 by
editions didier millet pte ltd
121 telok ayer street, #03-01
singapore 068590
telephone : +65 6324 9260
facsimile : +65 6324 9261
enquiries : edm@edmbooks.com.sg
website : www.edmbooks.com

first published in great britain 2007 by
kuperard
59 hutton grove, london n12 8ds
telephone : +44 (0) 20 8446 2440
facsimile : +44 (0) 20 8446 2441
enquiries : sales@kuperard.co.uk
website : www.kuperard.co.uk

Kuperard is an imprint of Bravo Ltd.

Printed in Singapore.

isbn: 978-185-7334-12-8

COVER CAPTIONS:

1 AND 2: Valsabbion is one of the newest purveyors of style in Istria.
3: Staggered Zagreb building façades.
4: An inviting outdoor pool.
5 AND PAGE 6: Pebble beaches make for clear, unclouded waters.
6: Zagorje church's Baroque cupola.
7: Vineyards abound in Istria.
8 AND PAGE 2: Visovac island's monastery ringed by green cypresses.
9, 19, 20 AND 21: The hotels of Suncani Hvar, new and exciting developments.
10: Croatia is a favourite with boaters.
11 AND THIS PAGE: Intricate architecture reflects the cultural influences at play.
12: A tempting dish at Valsabbion.
13: A Dalmatian in Dalmatia.
14: A small harbour along the coast.
15: The many coves and inlets of Hvar.
16 AND PAGE 4: The streets are paved in stone as smooth and shiny as marble.
17: Yachting—a popular activity.
18: Onofrio's fountain in Dubrovnik.

PAGE 8 AND 9: Dubrovnik, the undisputed pearl of the Adriatic, emerges in a pink halo of light at sunrise.

contents

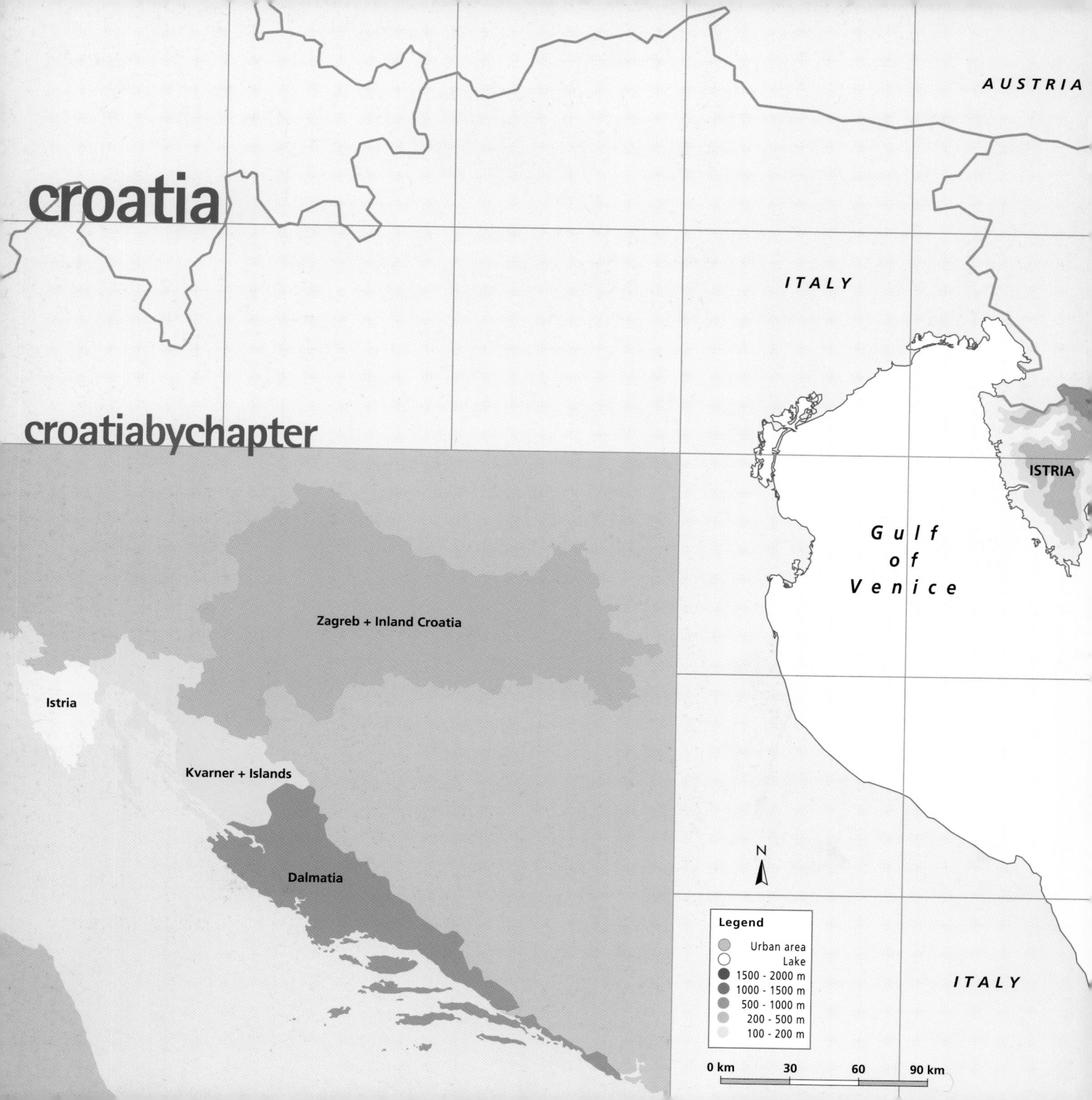

croatia

croatiabychapter

Zagreb + Inland Croatia

Istria

Kvarner + Islands

Dalmatia

AUSTRIA

ITALY

ISTRIA

Gulf of Venice

ITALY

N

Legend
- ◯ Urban area
- ◯ Lake
- 1500 - 2000 m
- 1000 - 1500 m
- 500 - 1000 m
- 200 - 500 m
- 100 - 200 m

0 km   30   60   90 km

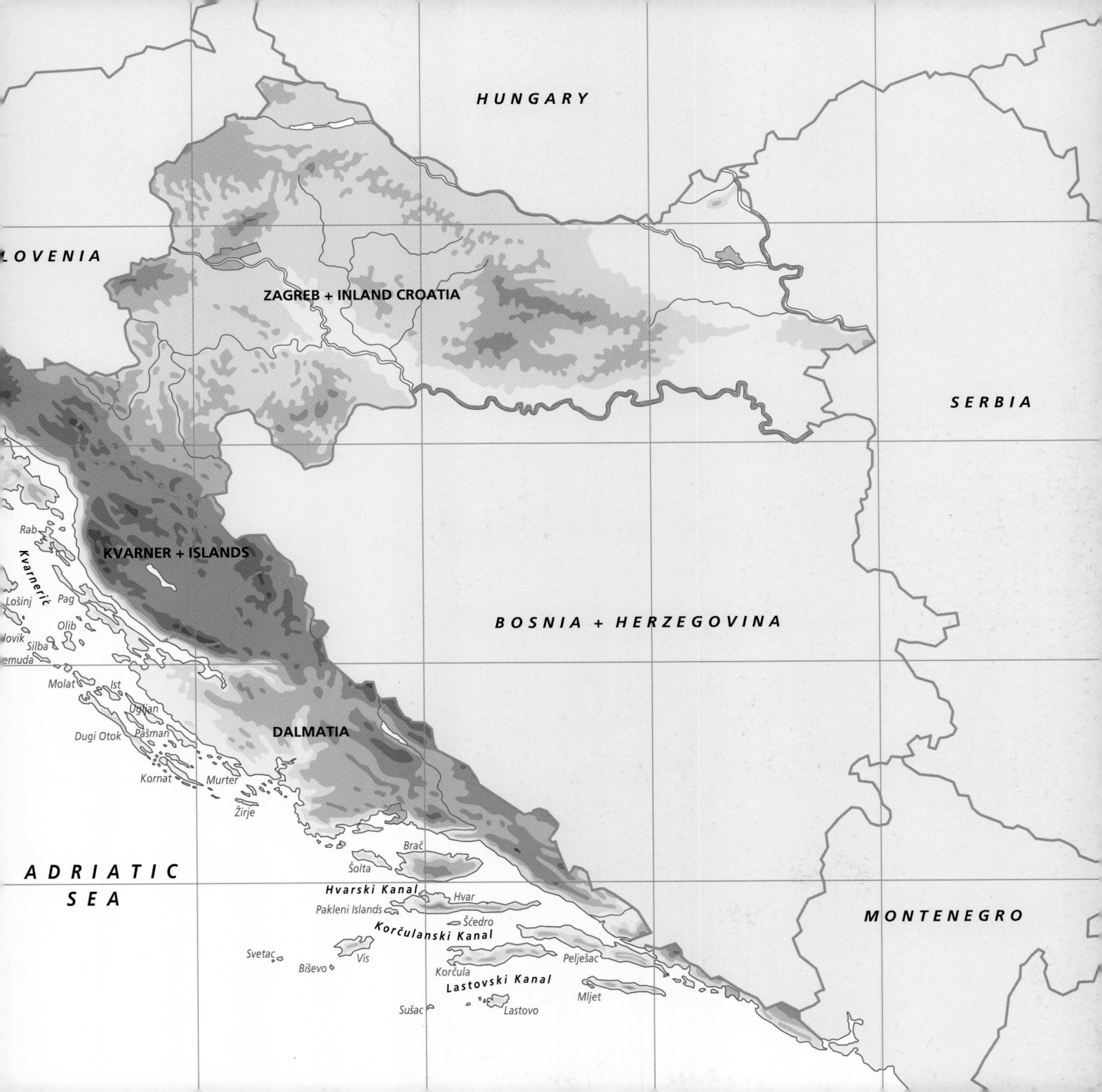

HUNGARY

SLOVENIA

ZAGREB + INLAND CROATIA

SERBIA

Rab

Kvarnerić

Lošinj
Pag

KVARNER + ISLANDS

Olib

Novik
Silba

emuda

BOSNIA + HERZEGOVINA

Molat
Ist

Uglian

Dugi Otok
Pašman

DALMATIA

Kornat
Murter

Žirje

Brač

Šolta

ADRIATIC
SEA

Hvarski Kanal

Pakleni Islands
Hvar

Svetac
Šćedro

Korčulanski Kanal

Biševo
Vis

Korčula
Lastovski Kanal

Pelješac

Sušac
Lastovo

Mljet

MONTENEGRO

introduction

the origins of the croatian people

Croatia has long been the ideal holiday destination, all deep blue sky and shimmering turquoise sea. Its Paleolithic inhabitants must have instinctively sensed its present-day potential or something similar when they took refuge there many eons ago. As, later, did the ancestors of the Croatian people, a mixed group of tribes and warring pagan hordes of Indo-European origin who were collectively known as the Illyrians (otherwise referred to as Istrians, Dalmatians and Liburnians, depending on where they settled). The name 'Croatian' is of Persian origin and first appeared in the 7th century.

During the Bronze Age, around the 12th century BCE, the nomads migrated west until they reached the Mediterranean. These 'barbarians', accustomed as they were to the harsh landscapes of the hinterland, suddenly found themselves exposed to the gentleness and beauty of the Dalmatian coast, and face to face with the infinite vastness of the ocean.

successive invasions

Throughout this period, other sea-faring people were busy settling down in various parts of the Mediterranean. Skilful navigators, traders and warriors, they were each and every one equally determined to stake their claim to the coastline.

During the 6th century BCE, Greek colonies made numerous incursions into Illyrian territory in search of better trading posts along the eastern Adriatic coast. In the 5th century BCE, invading Celts forced the Illyrians to retreat southwards to present-day Albania; and throughout the 4th century BCE, the Greeks continued their rapid and aggressive colonisation of the Adriatic coast, founding, among others, the cities of Issa (Vis), Pharos (Hvar), Tragurion (Trogir) and Epidaurum (Cavtat).

And then came the Romans. After two stubborn centuries of fiery resistance, the last Illyrian king, Genthius, was overthrown in 168 BCE by the legions of Caesar, and his people were forced to submit to the rule of the Roman Empire.

OPPOSITE: *Just inside the entrance to the old town of Dubrovnik, the 15th-century stone circular fountain of Onofrio provides a welcome resting place for those who wish to quench their thirst.*

THIS PAGE: *The indented coastline of Solta resembles a jagged frieze.*

five centuries of domination by the romans

Once the Dalmatian coast had been conquered and the province of Illyricum assimilated and reorganised, the Roman legions headed off into the interior intending to overthrow the 'barbarian' tribes whom they pursued as far as the Danube before finally managing to subjugate them. The Roman Empire thus expanded to encompass the whole of the Dalmatia region and inland Croatia, with its administrative capital in Salona (Solin).

Five centuries of Roman rule did not pass without leaving its mark: magnificent old stone ruins; cities such as Polensium (Pula), Jadera (Zadar) and especially Spalato (Split); Roman roads, some of which can still be seen throughout the Croatian countryside; the remains of thermal baths, temples, amphitheatres and stately villas.

As the Roman Empire was declining, towards the end of the 3rd century, Dalmatia produced her own Roman emperor, Diocletian. Born in the city of Salona in 236 CE, he was crowned emperor in 285 CE. His palace in Split was built in the image of his greatness and power and is today visited by thousands of tourists each year.

The division of the Roman Empire into Eastern and Western empires in 395 CE by the sons of the last Roman leader, Theodosius the Great, was highly significant for events to come. This division was echoed in 1054 by Christianity's Great Schism, which divided the Byzantine Church in the east, based in Constantinople, from the Catholic Church in the west, based in Rome, to which Croatia remained faithful.

slavs and croats

At the beginning of 600 CE, it was the turn of the Slavs. They started moving south across the Carpathian Mountains. Among their number were the Croats, who settled inland, west of the great divide. They organised themselves into communities and converted to Christianity. The foundations of a Croatian kingdom were laid by Prince Tomislav (910–928) and consolidated by Petar Kresimir (1058–1075) and his successor Dmitar Zvonimir (1075–1089). Ordained King of Croatia by Pope Gregory VII, Dmitar, who had no heir, was forced to form an alliance with the King of Hungary, who thus

THIS PAGE (FROM TOP): Columns in a Franciscan Monastery cloister; an outsize contemporary portrait of the Roman Emperor Diocletian on a wall in the old city of Split.

OPPOSITE: Grandiose Roman ruins can be found throughout much of Croatia, especially in the old Roman settlements in Dalmatia.

...magnificent old stone ruins...

became recognised as the legitimate sovereign of Croatia and Dalmatia, exerting control over his lands through a ban (viceroy), a sabor (parliament) and, of course, military forces. A tribal system had now become a feudal one.

dalmatia, a sought-after bride

Dalmatia provides access to the Adriatic for the whole of Central Europe. The Hungarians much desired this access and traversed the whole of northern Croatia in order to gain it. The Byzantines, however, also had their eye on Dalmatia. The Venetians came from the other side of the Adriatic, attacking Biograd and the surrounding islands, besieging the city of Zadar, which, despite heroic resistance, fell in 1202. Then came Mongol armies from the cold steppes of Central Asia, forcing the King of Hungary to retreat to Trogir.

Then, utmost confusion and anarchy reigned. Failing to maintain any real power, Croatia's aristocracy swayed with the arbitrary wind. Zadar was finally sold to Venice in 1409 for the paltry sum of 100,000 ducats in order to fill the state coffers. This development enabled La Serenissima to lord it over the entire Dalmatian coast, from Zadar to Ragusa (Dubrovnik), until 1797 when Napoleon conquered Venice.

the threat from the east

By the late 1500s, the Ottoman Empire was once again threatening Croatia. Having conquered Constantinople in 1453, the Ottomans spent the next decade bringing Bosnia to its knees, executing the country's last king, Stjepan Tomasevic, in 1463.

THIS PAGE (FROM TOP): The streets of Zadar hug the city walls, as if still wary of marauding invaders coming in from the sea, as was very common in the olden days; in Split, Venetian stone lions still stand on guard over the ancient remains of Diocletian's palace.

OPPOSITE: Dubrovnik glows with its rows of swaying palm trees and its mild Mediterranean climate.

Fearing the worst, the Austrians, who by 1527 had a Hapsburg ruler on the thrones of both Hungary and Croatia, decided to construct a string of fortresses in the region south of Zagreb in order to create a physical buffer zone against the Ottomans along its eastern frontier.

The Humanist elites along the Adriatic coast reacted firmly in the face of Eastern proselytising, strengthening their bonds with Western Christianity and its culture, and choosing to remain faithful to their Austro-Hungarian overlords.

eight years of napoleonic reign

The French presence in Dalmatia lasted from 1806 to 1814. The first stirrings of independence were felt in Split and along the Dalmatian coast.

After the Battle of Austerlitz in 1805, Austria was forced to cede Venice, Istria and Dalmatia to France. The Adriatic, including the ports of Trieste and Rijeka, was of great strategic importance to Napoleon, who viewed them as the perfect naval bases from which to enter the Balkans and beyond, in his move towards his ultimate goal, the East.

Under French administration, and the rule of General Auguste Marmont, Duke of Ragusa, Dalmatia was bathed in European ideas and the philosophies of the Encyclopedists. The Croatian

language was revived, along with a sense of patriotism. Schools were opened, the civil code introduced, and roads built, something that had not occurred since Roman times. With Napoleon retreating from Russia, however, the French left Zadar and withdrew from Dalmatia in 1814.

the illyrian movement

Educated Dalmatians traditionally spoke Italian, while German and Hungarian were spoken in the northern regions, emphasising the division between the Italianate coast and the Hungarian-dominated interior. By the 1930s, Dalmatians were tired of belonging to another culture; they wanted their own, and for the next two decades their search for an identity was expressed via the Illyrian movement. The sabor (parliament) supported the teaching of Croatian, a Slavic language, in schools, and the reunification of Dalmatia and Slavonia. However, this dream was quashed by the Austrian chancellor, Metternich, who refused to grant his Slavic subjects further autonomy.

the austro-hungarian empire: a double-headed eagle

With the creation of the Austro-Hungarian dual monarchy in 1867, the schism in Croatia grew ever deeper. By the late 19th century, this was echoed in the emergence of two quite distinct political movements. On the one hand, the National Party, borne out of the old Illyrian movement, led by Bishop Josip Juraj Strossmayer who dreamed of creating a Yugoslavian state within the Austro-Hungarian Empire. On the other, the Party of Rights, led by Ante Starčević, who aspired to an independent Croatia uniting Slavonia, Dalmatia, Istria, Slovenia and parts of Bosnia and Herzegovina.

In 1871, the uprising in Rakovia, led by the patriot Eugen Kvatrenik, marked the first popular resistance. In 1873, Ivan Mazuranic, ban (viceroy) of Croatia and an intellectual, undertook to modernise his country, founding the university and imposing obligatory lay schooling for all.

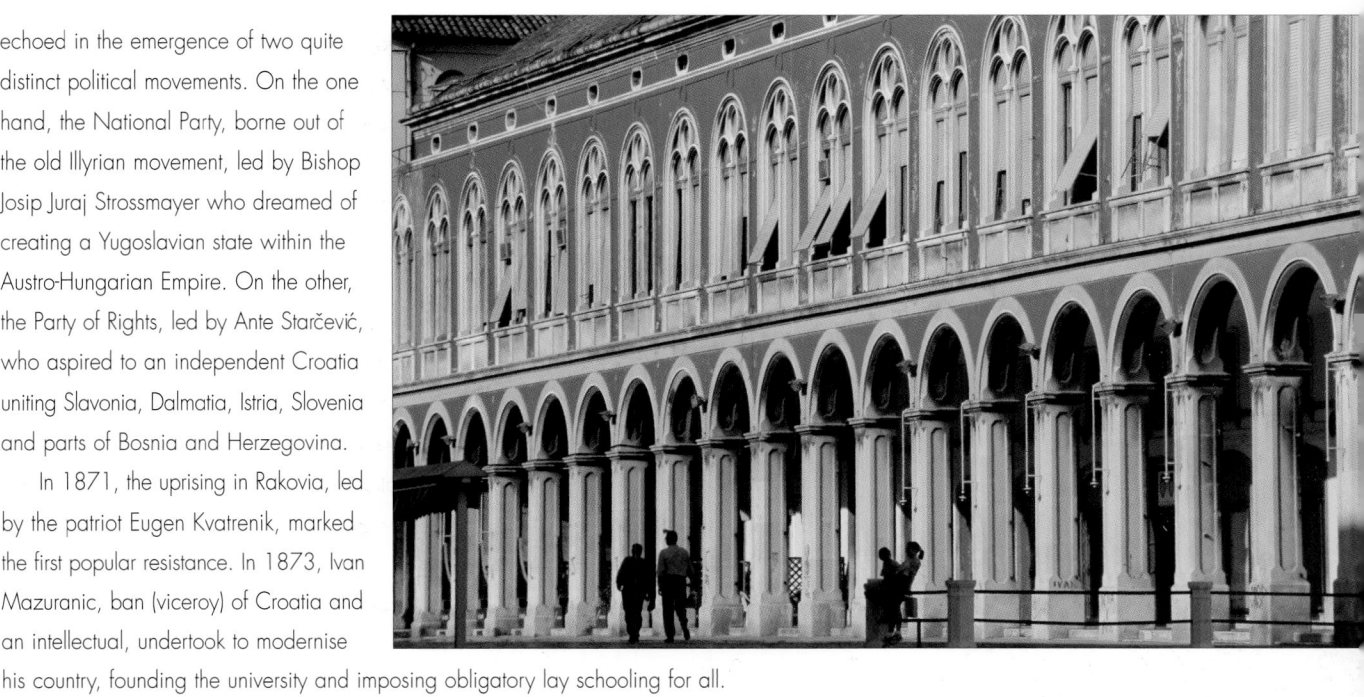

In 1878, the Congress of Berlin began the process of Turkish withdrawal from the Balkans. Three new independent kingdoms came into being: Romania, Serbia and Montenegro. In 1904, the Seljacka Stranka (Peasant Party) was formed by the Radic brothers, which subsequently became the Hrvatska Seljacka Stranka (the Croatian Peasant Party) in 1925. In 1908, Bosnia was annexed by the Austrian-Hungarian Empire.

the kingdom of yugoslavia

The assassination of Archduke Franz Ferdinand of Hapsburg in Sarajevo in 1914 by the Serb Gavrilo Princip sparked off the First World War. The following year, a handful of exiled Slovenian, Croat and Serbian politicians formed the Yugoslav Committee and drew up the foundations for a joint Yugoslav state.

OPPOSITE: Within the city walls, the town of Split has been built on and with the ruins of Diocletian's palace—a veritable city-museum.

THIS PAGE: The elegant symmetry of the neo-Renaissance arcaded façades surrounding the square imbue Split with a Venetian air.

After the collapse of the Austro-Hungarian Empire in 1918, the Yugoslav Committee became the National Council of Slovenes, Croats and Serbs, and it was soon able to negotiate the creation of the longed-for kingdom, with its capital in Belgrade. This was opposed by Stjepan Radiç who, while agreeing with the idea of Yugoslavia itself, preferred to make it a federal democracy. With civil war brewing, Radiç was brutally assassinated, leaving the way open for King Aleksandar I to proclaim a royal dictatorship in 1929, and the Kingdom of Yugoslavia.

the ustaše party and the second world war

In 1934, King Aleksandar was himself openly assassinated on the streets of Marseilles while on a rare diplomatic visit by a member of the Internal Macedonian Revolutionary Organisation, with the complicity of the Croatian Ustaše party.

When Germany invaded Yugoslavia on 6 April 1941, it immediately installed the fascist Ustaše party, with the support of Mussolini's Italy. Between the decisive war years of 1941 and 1945, thousands upon thousands of Jews, Roma and Serbian political opponents were exterminated.

tito and the partisans

During this period, the Croat Josip Broz, better known as Tito, headed the anti-fascist resistance throughout the entire country. In 1944, with the help of the Red Army, Tito summarily seized power and ruled the whole of Yugoslavia, its six republics and single Communist party, for 35 years with an iron fist. Upon his death in 1980, all the old tensions came rising up to the surface again. In Kosovo, which is largely Muslim, a rise of Serbian nationalism led to a bloody and drawn-out repression of the population. After having founded the extreme right-wing

party Hrvatska Demokratska Zajednica, Franjo Tudjman had himself elected President of the Republic of Croatia in 1990, while Slobodan Milosevic came to power in Belgrade.

croatian independence

In the face of the violent events taking place in Kosovo, the Slovenians and Croats both declared their independence in 1991, exerting their right to self-government as stated in the Yugoslavian Constitution. Milosevic's Yugoslavian army wasted no time in reacting. The rift between the Serbs and Croats was now out in the open, signalling the start of a terrible war of territorial conquest and massive destruction. The desperate resistance put up by the town of Vukovar in Slavonia is still deeply emblazoned in the memory of all those who were involved or affected, as are all the atrocities that ensued.

The Dayton Accord, signed in Paris in 1995, signified an end to the fighting. After the death of President Tudjman, Croatia moved towards installing a democratic regime and becoming a member of the European Union. Political alternation came into being. In January 2000, a centre-left coalition was formed around the Social-Democrat Prime Minister Ivica Racan. The following month, Stjepan Mesic was elected President of the Republic. In November 2003, the victory of the conservatives and the nomination of Ivo Sanader as head of government, followed by the re-election of President Stjepan Mesic for a further five years. The next elections will be held in 2010.

a horseshoe

Present-day Croatia lies at the heart of Europe. Zagreb is close to Vienna, Berlin, Venice, Ljubljana and Belgrade. It shares 2,028 km (1,260 miles) of land frontiers with six other nations: Italy, a border to the north with Slovenia and Hungary, Serbia to the east, and

OPPOSITE (FROM TOP): The statue of the Ban Josip Jelačića, Zagreb's famed viceroy, dominates the city square bearing the same name; a wall erected in memory of the victims of the Yugoslavian war—each brick bears a victim's name.

THIS PAGE: A clear aerial view of Zagreb's Umjetnicki Pavilion, housing various contemporary art exhibitions, and its grounds, designed in the style of French landscaped lawns and gardens.

THIS PAGE (FROM TOP): *The idyllic postcard image of Bol's long sandy beach entices bathers; Modra Spilja, the lovely blue grotto on the island of Bisevo.*

OPPOSITE (FROM TOP): *Sardine fishing is back in action in Istria's ports; Istria's lush interior lends itself perfectly to green tourism.*

Bosnia and Herzegovina and Montenegro to the south. This strategic position was not long ago Croatia's Achilles' heel. Croatia's shape is likened to a horseshoe, but one can easily see similarities to the Winged Victory of Samothrace, facing west. While this comparison seems far-fetched, it does conjure up Croatia's dual personality and East-West divide.

a small country with a long coastline

Croatia has 1,778 km (1,105 miles) of mainland coastline, together with 1,185 islands and islets within its territory, making a total of 5,835 km (3,626 miles) for a surface area of 56,538 sq km (21,829 sq miles). Ten per cent of this surface area consists of 450 preservation zones, the pride of the country's natural heritage. If one adds to this all the maritime areas also under protection, Croatia has a total of 6,129 sq km (2,366 sq miles) of ecologically protected zones.

a gift of nature

There are eight national parks, including those of Plitvice, Kornati, Brijuni, and northern Velebit, as well as 10 natural parks and two highly protected natural reserves, Bijela and Samarska in the Bjelolasica range, and Rosanski and Hadjduk Kukovi in the Velebit range.

There are 430 zones with strict rules concerning the protection of their flora and fauna: *777 known species of animals*, including wolves, brown bears and lynxes living in the dense fir forests, extremely rich fishing resources, and *44 different varieties of plants*, including *Pinguicula Alpina* (a type of iris) from Gorski Kotar, and Centaury, which are increasingly rare and proud national emblems for Croatia.

the pannonian plain

To the north of the country lies a vast plain, the Pannonian plain. It is irrigated by the Sava, the Drava and the Danube, and culminates in Slavonia with the Papuk Mountains and the Medvednica range overlooking Zagreb from a height of 1,030 m (3,379 ft). Heavily influenced by Austro-Hungarian culture, the region is essentially rural, with the exception of the industrial basin around the capital.

the adriatic coast

Croatia's Adriatic coastline is composed of Istria, the Kvarner Gulf, and Dalmatia, with mountain ranges inland and numerous islands dotted along its entire length, with a typically Mediterranean climate throughout. It possesses no fewer than five UNESCO World Heritage Sites: Poreč, Sibenik, Trogir, Split and Dubrovnik.

and the mountains in between

Linking the Adriatic littoral and the Pannonian plain lie the high plateaux of the Lika and the Dinaric Alps, which culminate at 1,831 m (6,007 ft). This mountainous barrier includes the karst range to the north and all the rivers that flow into the Adriatic to the south. Despite being sparsely populated, its agricultural land is meticulously farmed.

a latin temperament in a slav body: croatia and europe

According to the writer and historian Gregory Péroche, 'Croatia has been part of Western Europe rather than the Balkans since the 7th century.' Croatia first applied for membership of the European Union on 20 February 2003. This was officially validated by the European Parliament the following year and is set to come into being in 2009. According to the nation-wide polls, approximately half of Croatia's population is in favour of this move.

a cultural mosaic

Croatia has been invaded too many times to count—the playground of the Roman and Byzantine Empires, the Republic of Venice and Austro-Hungarian rulers. Its lands have been annexed, and divided up between foreign kingdoms, reduced to a handful of despoiled cities, torn apart, lost and re-conquered. Barbarians, Greeks, Romans, Turks, Venetians, Austrians, Byzantines, Mongol hordes and Napoleonic armies have all trampled its soil, each leaving their mark but also a trail of destruction. Each of these peoples has imposed its culture and beliefs, its language and customs on the local population. This turmoil has left its scars and memories, but it is these histories and this multiculturalism that have forged the country's identity and heritage. Only now is Croatia able to start writing its own history.

a young state for an old nation

It was only 15 years ago, in 1991, that Croatia gained its independence. It is a young country with a young population: 17 per cent of the population of around 5 million are under 15 years of age. The country has embarked upon a vast and highly ambitious programme of reconstruction. Within the space of four years, half the destroyed real estate has been rebuilt. Great importance has been given to economic growth—the average GDP growth rate is 6 per cent—particularly in the sectors of metallurgy, ship-building and the food industry, as well as the more traditional sectors of fishing and fish-processing, which are estimated to handle 24,000 tonnes per year.

tourism

Tourism is a major source of income for Croatia, and it is growing all the time, with 8 million tourists in 2003, and 8.4 million in 2005. With the gradual move towards an opening up of the country's market economy, both Croat and foreign investments in the hotel sector are on a steeply rising gradient. Gone is the era of vast state-owned hotel complexes, which seem slightly out of step with the more selective, largely foreign clientele. While outdoor camping or trekking holidays and organised group coach tours still play an important part in the country's tourist industry, the trend is towards more independent tourism, more luxurious accommodation and better infrastructure.

A sudden proliferation of small-scale, carefully-restored country houses, seaside hotels, spas, and regional gourmet restaurants is springing up almost overnight; old houses are being snatched up for renovation and restoration by private investors; bed-and-breakfast accommodation options and forays into green tourism are both growing rapidly in numbers. Alongside the traditional 'room for rent' signs outside people's houses in the rural villages, rental agencies have an increasing number of elegant villas boasting pools and sea views in their books.

the new wave

Cruises, and especially leisure sailing, are becoming increasingly popular along the scenic coastal regions, with both locals and visitors. Croatia now has 50 or so marinas, with quite a number of them either recently refurbished or newly created, with boat

OPPOSITE (FROM TOP): The stunning Velika Kapela mountain range; vineyards abound and thrive in the Pljevisica region's climate.
THIS PAGE (FROM TOP): Every single self-respecting seafood restaurant in Croatia will offer the day's catch, fresh from the Adriatic; a naïve landscape painting makes the perfect souvenir.

hire companies and agencies constantly setting up in business along the Adriatic coastline. With the rising demand for yachting holidays, there is definitely more than enough of a market for them; the competition serves to raise standards, and business is booming. The French leisure-boat construction company Jeanneau, for example, has five separate bases in Croatia. The future of the country's tourism undoubtedly lies in the diversity of its landscapes and culture, and in protecting them while continuing to develop suitably controlled infrastructure and quality accommodation.

croatia's illustrious figures

Throughout history and in contemporary times, Croatia has produced a great number of famous people who have made a series of highly significant contributions in a myriad of fields ranging from the arts and sciences to academia and sports.

Picasso's muse, Dora Maar, whose real name was Theodora Markovic, was the daughter of a Zagreb architect. The famous American novelist Ernest Hemingway's sometime muse was a beautiful Croat called Adriana Ivancic, who is supposed to have inspired the character of the Contessa Renata in *Across the River and into the*

Trees, published in 1950. The renowned Hollywood actor John Malkovich, and Goran Visnjic, star of the hit US television series *ER*, as well as Branco Lustig, producer of the award-winning film *Schindler's List*, are all acclaimed natives of Croatia.

The invention of the modern-day parachute is attributed to one Faust Vrancic, also known as Veranzio, a native of Sibenik, in his book *Machinae Novae* first published in 1595. Rudjer Boskovic, a prominent Jesuit scholar and native of Dubrovnik, was the 18th-century precursor of today's atomic theory. Ivan Lupis perfected the first torpedo, in 1866, in Rijeka, not long after Joseph Ressel, from Motovun in Istria, had invented the ship's mechanical propeller. Slavoljub Penkala dreamed up the famous fountain pen in 1907. The world's first rigid airship was the work of the Zagreb inventor, David Schwartz, whose revolutionary designs were subsequently sold to Count von Zeppelin. The criminologist Ivan Vucetic was responsible, in 1920, for inventing the technique of fingerprinting, still in use today. Two Croats have been awarded the Nobel Prize for Chemistry, Lavoslav Ruzicka in 1939 and Vladimir Prelog in 1975, while Nikola Tesla, a Croat-American physicist dedicated his life to understanding electricity, and he was credited as inventing the radio. Mirko Grmek, the physicist-historian, developed the concept of pathogenesis in his *History of AIDS*, and the geneticist Miroslav Radman won the Grand Prix de l'Inserm in 2003 for his contribution to genetics and molecular biology.

OPPOSITE: Island cruises and sailing are counted among Croatia's most flourishing activities, and boat-hire companies and marinas do brisk business in this area.

THIS PAGE (FROM TOP): Picasso's portrait of Dora Maar, a Croat who was one of the artist's muses; Hollywood actor John Malkovich, originally of Croatian extraction; football fans proudly display the Croatian team colours of red and white at an international match.

Croats have also excelled in sport. At the 1996 Olympic Games, Croatia won gold medals for handball and water-polo, while Janica Kostelic won three gold medals and a silver for downhill skiing at the 2002 Winter Olympics in Salt Lake City. Gordan Kozulj (gold medallist in the European Swimming Championships, Berlin 2002) and Sanja Jovanovic (bronze medallist in the European Swimming Championships, Madrid 2004) are both world-class sportswomen, and Goran Ivanisevic, 2001 Wimbledon champion, remains a top male tennis player. Stipe Bozic is one of the world's most successful mountaineers, with Mount Everest under his belt on two separate occasions.

a tie with france

The tie, that famous fashion accessory, is Croat in origin ('cravate' from 'Croat' or 'Hvrat' in Croatian). It was introduced to the French court of Louis XIV by the Croat cavalrymen who wore red ribbons knotted at their necks. The courtiers adopted the habit and it soon became de rigueur, and has remained so to this day. As the writer Oscar Wilde once said: 'A well-tied tie is the first serious step in life.'

religious art and the cult of the virgin

The Greeks and the Romans venerated the goddess of beauty, Aphrodite and Venus. In early Christendom, Paleochristian art in Dalmatia and Istria reflected the cult of the Virgin. A mosaic in the Euphrasian basilica in Poreč shows Mary sitting in Christ's place.

The Middle Ages brought prosperity to Croatia and from the 11th to 15th centuries, a string of churches, basilicas and cathedrals was built, giving artistic expression to the fervent religious sentiment of the time. Links with the Byzantine tradition were not, however, altogether lost. Panel paintings from the period illustrate the Crucifixion in a realistic way, as in traditional Byzantine art. A similar realism is seen in altarpieces such as those in the Church of All Saints in Korčula that depict the Virgin and Child flanked by saints. The cult of the Virgin flourished throughout the Renaissance, until the end of the 16th century, but it is still seen today in the pilgrimage of Our Lady of Trsat on the hill above Rijeka.

THIS PAGE (FROM TOP): *Detail of stone carvings in Šibenik's St James' Cathedral, a fine masterpiece of traditional Croatian religious art; Croatian architecture reflects the use of religious imagery and motifs in the everyday, such as in the crosses on these town roofs.*

OPPOSITE: *The Baroque cupola of Zagorje church is a beautiful example of religious art.*

...from the 11th to 15th centuries, a string of churches, basilicas and cathedrals was built...

zagreb+inlandcroatia

Austria

Slovenia

Hungary

Serbia

Čakovec

Varaždin
Varaždin

Ivanšćica
1061

Koprivnica

Krapina

Krapina-Zagorje

643

Virovitica

Osijek-Baranja

Sljeme
1035

Bjelovar

Slatina

*Kroprivnica
Kritževci*

ZAGREB

Bjevolar-Bilogora

Osijek

Trdinov vrh
1181

Velika
Gorica

Čazma

s l a v o n i a

Zagreb

Humka
489

Daruvar

Papuk
953

Našice

Vukovar

Kaptol

Karlovac
Duga Resa

Sisak

Požega-Slavonia

Požega

Đakovo

Vinkovci

985

Petrinja

Vukovar-Syrmia

Glina

Nova Gradiška

Sisak-Moslavina

Brod-Posavina

Slavonski
Brod

Ogulin

Kostajnica
615

Hrvatska
Kostajnica

Županja

Karlovac

Dvor

Slunj

Gunja

Plaški

N

> The Regent Esplanade
> Euromarine

**Kvarner +
Islands**

Bosnia + Herzegovina

Dalmatia

Legend	
≡	Highways
▬	Main roads
—	Other roads
⋮⋮⋮	Proposed road
══	Road under construction
⊕	Airport
●	Urban area
○	Lake
●	1500 - 2000 m
●	1000 - 1500 m
●	500 - 1000 m
●	200 - 500 m
●	100 - 200 m

0 km   20   40   60 km

zagreb, the capital

If one is to begin with the definitives, then it must be said that the one place to stay in Zagreb is the Esplanade Hotel. One can picture Agatha Christie arriving on the Orient Express and walking the short distance from the station to the hotel on foot, admiring King Tomislav Square along the way. The buildings around the square are perfect examples of the Austro-Hungarian style of the period, their façades painted in the pale yellow so fashionable in Vienna at that time. The Esplanade, now known as the Regent Esplanade, is as elegant as it ever was, thanks to its superb restoration.

The main square, Trg Bana Josip Jelačića, is the hub for most of the city's trams and divides the old town from the new. The writer Lawrence Durrell recalls the square fondly as having pretty turn-of-the-century buildings, light brown in colour, with florist stands and peasants selling traditionally embroidered wares. The upper and lower towns are connected by a funicular built in 1889, which is still very much in common use.

Kaptol, the ecclesiastical district, is still mostly dominated by the Cathedral of the Assumption of the Blessed Virgin Mary. Very little remains of the original Romanesque church, which at one stage was converted into stables by the Mongols. Repeatedly rebuilt and restored, subsequent Ottoman invasions saw the removal of the famous spires of its Gothic successor, and an ill-timed earthquake in 1880 damaged most of the remaining structure. The last major restoration programme was undertaken at the turn of the 20th century by the famous Austrian architect Herman Bollé. Inside, the quietly inspiring cathedral is a sanctuary for the tombs of famous Croats.

Bollé also created another of Zagreb's key monuments, the Mirogoj cemetery. Widely considered to be one of the most beautiful cemetery parks in Europe and built on a scale to match, it is surrounded by an immense arcade with shaded alleys where famous Croatians such as Vatroslav Lisinski, Ljudevit Gaj and Stjepan Radić lie.

Until the 19th century, Tkalciceva Street was a stream running through the middle of the city, dividing the Kaptol and Gradec districts. Today it is paved over, but still has a somewhat medieval and bucolic atmosphere, with low, pastel-coloured houses,

PAGE 30: The superb geometry of Bana Josip Jelačića Square.

OPPOSITE: Zagreb's main square with the great statue of Ban Josip Jelačića on horseback

THIS PAGE (FROM TOP): A fine example of late 19th-century façades; colourful trams are still very much in use as public transport.

carved wooden balconies and patches of garden, and grass cropping up here and there between the paving stones. The cafés and shops that have taken over the ground floors of these houses have not, so far, affected this village atmosphere. Through the narrow alleyways climbing up to the Gradec district in the upper town, one soon finds oneself surrounded by palaces, former convents, churches and museums, from where there is a splendid panoramic view over the lower town.

a patchwork landscape

The unspoilt countryside of the Samobor region to the west and the Varaždin region to the north stretches as far as the Slovenian border. Around Zagreb, lush green hills are topped by ruined castles, and vestiges of ancient fortresses with crenellated towers and drawbridges. From the 12th century onwards, these structures formed Western Europe's buffer against successive invasions by the Tatars and Turks. Trakoscan Castle looks for all the world like it has come straight out of a fairytale, while Veliki Tabor Castle is a fine example of military architecture.

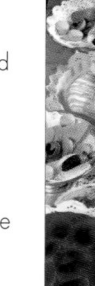

Buildings with baroque art and in the Rococo style flourished in the plains of the Drava and Sava rivers, inspired by the architecture of Hungarian and Austrian cities. The palaces, churches and monuments of the town of Varaždin compete with one another for colour, decoration and imagination. Ornate French pastries, delicately arranged, are proudly on display within the tearooms. The famous mille-feuilles from the small town of Samobor are reputed to lure many a Zagreb resident from his home on Sundays.

The countryside is a gently undulating and peaceful stretch, where cultivated fields give way to verdant pastures and vineyards. Marshy meadows lined with poplars are home to countless Waders and other fauna. The landscape is cloaked in browns, whites, greens and reds depending on the seasons, like a quaint patchwork.

THIS PAGE (FROM TOP): The luminous cupola of the city's Art Pavilion; delicate pastries from Samobor; fountains are a symbol of the omnipresence of water in Zagreb.
OPPOSITE: The Zagreb region is dotted with castles, including the magnificent Trakoscan Castle.

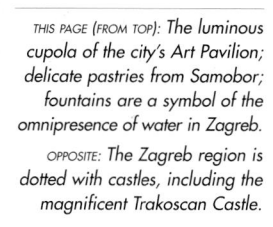

Around Zagreb, green hills are topped by ruined castles...

Further on, nearer the Slovenian border, the countryside becomes more forested, mostly with evergreen pines, and looks almost Tyrolean. The hamlets of this predominantly agricultural region are picturesque snapshots from another era come to life, dotted here and there with traditional wooden farmhouses hung about with garlands of maize.

The simplicity of this countryside and its people is charmingly echoed in the artistic compositions created by the community of peasant-artists around the village of Hlebine, near Varaždin. Its main street is lined with artisans' workshops and galleries exhibiting and selling the work of countless local artists, especially those of Ivan Generalić, the best-known exponent of Croatian naïve art. Other neighbouring villages that come in on this local artists' circuit include Molve, Koprivnica and Durdevac.

slavonia, little known land

Originally covered by the Pannonian sea, now traversed by the Drava, Sava and Danube rivers, Slavonia is a land comprised of one vast flat plain. The waters receded slowly over the millennia, uncovering the land inch by inch and leaving far behind them a seemingly endless, deserted horizon of fertile marshland and a convoluted maze of trickling streams and ancient forests, under a permanently dappled sky.

As early as 6,000 BCE, this fertile land, a crossroads for the migrating hordes of early man, proved irresistible to the nomadic tribes who settled there. Fascinating traces of Neolithic culture have been found at Vinkovci and several nearby sites, and pottery sherds from the prehistoric era have been unearthed at Vucedol.

LEFT: *In the naturalistic land of water and trees, the horse is king.*

OPPOSITE: *Fertile Slavonia is the wheat granary of Croatia.*

THIS PAGE: *The snow-covered steeple of Osijek Cathedral.*

Largely undiscovered by tourism, Slavonia has a staggeringly rich cultural and natural heritage.

Largely undiscovered by tourism, Slavonia has a staggeringly rich cultural and natural heritage. Its people have a long-standing and deep-rooted respect for tradition, founded in the rich land around them, their pastures, wheat fields and vineyards. Traminac, a wine produced in the region around Ilok, is of international renown. The local confectionery and chocolate from Požega, and Slatina's sparkling wine, are no less reputed. The local cuisine is particularly interesting and hearty, featuring specialities such as 'bregovski' (a thin layer of flaky pastry with apple, walnut and poppy seeds), carp with a cream sauce, 'perkelt' (a fish stew with paprika), and frogs' legs.

The domains of lords and princes were reserved for hunting. Deer, wild boar and other game abound in the region around Tikveš; and Eugene of Savoy, Friedrich of Hapsburg and Wilhelm II of Austria all used to organise royal hunting parties there. The extensive marshes are resting places for black swans, wild geese and various other migrating birds, and

spawning grounds for fish such as pike, carp and bream. The rivers provide sport and play for local and visiting fishermen, bathers and canoers, and on their banks lie the splendid old towns of Osijek and Vukovar (on the Danube and Drava rivers respectively), and the formidable fortress of Slavonski Brod (on the Sava river). The two spa towns of Požega and Pakra grew up alongside springs.

The beautiful town of Vukovar, on the Serbian border, found itself in the frontline of hostilities during the conflicts in the early 1990s. Delivered up to the gunfire and tanks

OPPOSITE: *Djakovo Cathedral is a landmark, rising up majestically from the flat Slavonian plains.*
THIS PAGE (FROM TOP): *At a bend in the Drava, Osijek shines out; Slavonia is home to various species of migratory birds.*

of the Yugoslav army, the town with its baroque palaces, art galleries and elegant churches was reduced to rubble, and its population suffered great loss. Its bridge was the site of some of the bloodiest confrontations that are still very much alive in memories. A memorial to those who fell in the conflict has been erected in the middle of the fields nearby. Today, Vukovar tends its wounds, rebuilding itself on a desolate wasteland.

plitvice and its lakes

Plitvice National Park is a UNESCO World Heritage Site and a favourite tourist destination for both Croats and foreigners alike. It is a vast forested domain, in the darkest corners of which feral wolves and wild cats are said to lurk.

At the heart of the park is a natural depression formed by 16 lakes that flow from the upper lake, at 637 m (2,090 ft), to the lower lake 134 m (440 ft) below via a series of pools and picturesque waterfalls. The water wends its way between carpets of moss, water lilies, ferns and limestone deposits.

In the calmer pools, the beautifully clear water reveals a subaquatic world of various types of fish swimming in and out of the tall wavering reflections of overhanging trees. In the company of skimming, dipping clusters of dragonflies, visitors take in the enchanting sights from the sides of canyons, skirt tumbling waterfalls and traverse bubbling whirlpools on wooden walkways, enveloped in a cool drizzle, to footpaths overlooking the untouched liquid turquoise surfaces of pools.

THIS PAGE (FROM TOP): The open war wounds of the martyred town of Vukovar, on the Danube, are still painfully visible after many years; the clear lakes of Plitvice are a natural reserve for wild trout.

OPPOSITE: The wooded walk around Plitvice's lakes is breathtaking.

PAGE 42 AND 43: The upper lakes cascade into the lower ones in a continuous, grandiose spectacle.

Plitvice National Park is a UNESCO World Heritage Site...

The Regent Esplanade

THIS PAGE (FROM TOP): *An opulently decorated room exhibits all the trademark luxury of The Regent; the classic 1920s-style Le Bistro exudes an understated glamour; the Esplanade 1925 lounge bar.*

OPPOSITE (FROM LEFT): *The imposing façade of The Regent Esplanade gleams in the afternoon sunlight; the grand Zinfandel's Restaurant serves modern fusion cuisine in a stylishly high-ceilinged room.*

Every great city has its great hotel—a landmark building that somehow epitomises the history, glamour and style of its location. In Singapore, it's Raffles Hotel; in Hong Kong, The Peninsula; in New York, The Plaza; in Paris, The Ritz…. And in Zagreb, capital of Croatia and the country's largest city, it's The Regent Esplanade.

Dating back to 1925, The Regent Esplanade is one of the most elegant and gracious buildings in Zagreb, and as the hub of the city's vibrant social life for more than eight decades it can count presidents, politicians, film stars and musicians among its many famous and distinguished guests.

The fact that the hotel has recently undergone a complete renovation, thereby adding a contemporary flavour to the old-world splendour, has only served to ensure that it will continue to provide the highest standards of hospitality, sophistication and luxury for many more years to come.

Nowhere are the results of this modernisation better illustrated than in the 209 bedrooms and suites—sumptuous sanctuaries where guests can relax in style. Similarly, bathrooms are havens of warm and sensuous escapism, while cutting-edge technology and the finest quality toiletries, linens and accessories are standard issue.

Although the hotel is located at the heart of this fascinating and historic city, guests will not have to go further than the hotel's restaurants for some of the finest dining experiences that can be had in the capital. Zinfandel's Restaurant is an elegant and very impressive old-fashioned dining room that has been tastefully modernised, and diners here will be offered dishes reflecting the gastronomic culture of the region as well as a selection of the finest Croatian and international wines. The Esplanade 1925 lounge and cocktail bar provides an intimate setting for relaxed conversations where light refreshments and various snacks are served throughout the day. At night it transforms effortlessly into a sophisticated lounge bar, the perfect place to relax after dinner with a classic cocktail in hand. The art deco interior of Le Bistro recaptures the simple elegance of a 1920s Parisian eating-house, which, besides serving the best strukli (a local variation of pastry made with fresh cheese) in town, also offers a wide selection of regional and seasonal dishes.

In addition, the hotel has a state-of-the-art fitness centre, a spa with a tempting range of exotic therapies and treatments and a casino as well as a grand ballroom with a capacity for up to 250 guests. Indeed, the hotel's very size, the variety of its function rooms and its central location in Zagreb, together with its vastly experienced staff, make it an excellent and memorable venue for business meetings or other social events such as banquets and weddings.

PHOTOGRAPHS COURTESY OF THE REGENT ESPLANADE.

FACTS		
	ROOMS	195 rooms • 13 suites • 1 presidential suite
	FOOD	Zinfandel's Restaurant: modern fusion • Le Bistro: regional
	DRINK	Esplanade 1925
	FEATURES	spa • gym • casino • ballroom
	BUSINESS	business centre • conference facilities
	NEARBY	National Theatre • Botanical Gardens • Archaeological Museum
	CONTACT	Mihanoviceva 1, 10000 Zagreb • telephone: +385.1.456 6666 • facsimile: +385.1.456 6020 • email: info.zagreb@rezidorregent.com • website: www.regenthotels.com

Euromarine

Croatia's Adriatic coastline is a peerless nautical paradise, its cerulean blue waters dramatically studded, jewel-like, with over a thousand islands. Considered by many to be a godsend for sailors seeking a glamorous and challenging holiday, its unparalleled coastline can only be properly experienced from the water. With a wide choice of sea-craft from the fleet of leading yacht charter company Euromarine, this is almost as easily done as said.

With almost 20 years of experience, Euromarine understand implicitly that one of the most satisfying ways of arriving at any destination is from the sea, whether it be under sail or motor. Detailed itineraries and adventure tours can be tailored to exact criteria, commencing from any one of Croatia's four major ports. Circular voyages can begin in Dubrovnik, Split, Biograd or Pula, each marina conveniently being within a short distance of the local airport.

Each one of these bustling cities has excellent public transport links, for easy access to Croatia's other attractions. One-way luxury boat charters are becoming increasingly popular, for indulgent days of cruising without the need to backtrack—the luxurious alternative to car rental.

For a truly leisurely marine experience, hand all responsibility over to a fully qualified skipper of a sleek, privately

chartered boat. Euromarine's friendly on-board staff will ensure that every voyage is a carefree and thoroughly enjoyable escape away from the quotidian. Seasoned sailors, however, might prefer to captain their own journey by going with the bareboat option. Sunbathing, reading, diving into fish-filled waters or simply taking in the sea-views are favourite diversions while on board.

THIS PAGE (CLOCKWISE FROM LEFT): With over 100 boats to choose from, Euromarine is well-equipped to handle a range of preferences; one of Euromarine's yachts out on the waters of the Adriatic; experienced sailors can choose to forego a hired crew and take themselves on a private journey.

OPPOSITE: Boats are fitted out with all modern conveniences and furnished to high standards, as befitting a luxurious holiday.

...every voyage is a carefree and enjoyable escape from the quotidian.

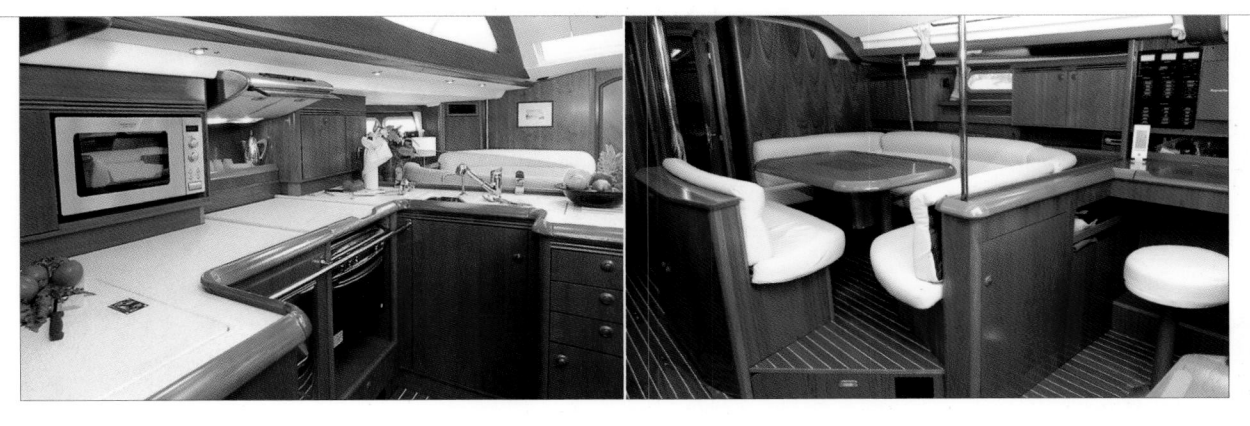

True sea lovers will revel in the laid-back balmy days and palmy bays on the way down towards Montenegro—the undisputed geographical star of the latest James Bond movie—softly buffeted by the warm breezes of the Mediterranean. The more adrenaline-driven, on the other hand, will much prefer the effortless acceleration of Jeanneau's Prestige 46 model. A fully fitted-out, thoroughbred boat uniting simplicity with performance, the Prestige 46 is built for speed and furnished in stylish elegance, delighting both extremes of impassioned connoisseur and appreciative layman.

With an impressive, gleaming fleet of over 100 vessels, Euromarine guarantee a boat to suit every need, with excellent back-up services en route for added reassurance. All yachts are equipped with cutting-edge safety and navigation equipment, with each boat finished to the highest standards of comfort and luxury. Journeys are made even smoother still with an airport transfer and complete yacht provisioning service.

Euromarine's fleet grows ever larger and more diverse as the world wakes up to Croatia's phenomenal appeal as a sailing destination. Its current range encompasses catamarans, glamorous motor yachts and state-of-the-art Sun Odyssey vessels, mostly from master craftsmen and boat designers, Jeanneau. These select high-calibre cruisers perfectly integrate open lounging areas and classically stylish interiors with the economy of space and modern efficiency demanded by today's discerning sailing fraternity.

Succumb to the lure of a sailing holiday this summer with a private exploration of the incomparable Adriatic coast. For confidence at sea and the utmost comfort at anchor, Croatia's most experienced boat charter company should be the first port of call.

FACTS

PRODUCTS	yacht rental • crew hire
FEATURES	over 100 vessels (mainly Jeanneau) • marinas (Pula, Biograd, Split, Dubrovnik)
SERVICES	airport–marina transfer • skipper and hostess service • provisioning
CONTACT	Svetice 15, 10000 Zagreb • telephone: +385.12.325 234 • facsimile: +385.12.325 237 • email: charter@euromarine.hr • website: www.euromarine.hr

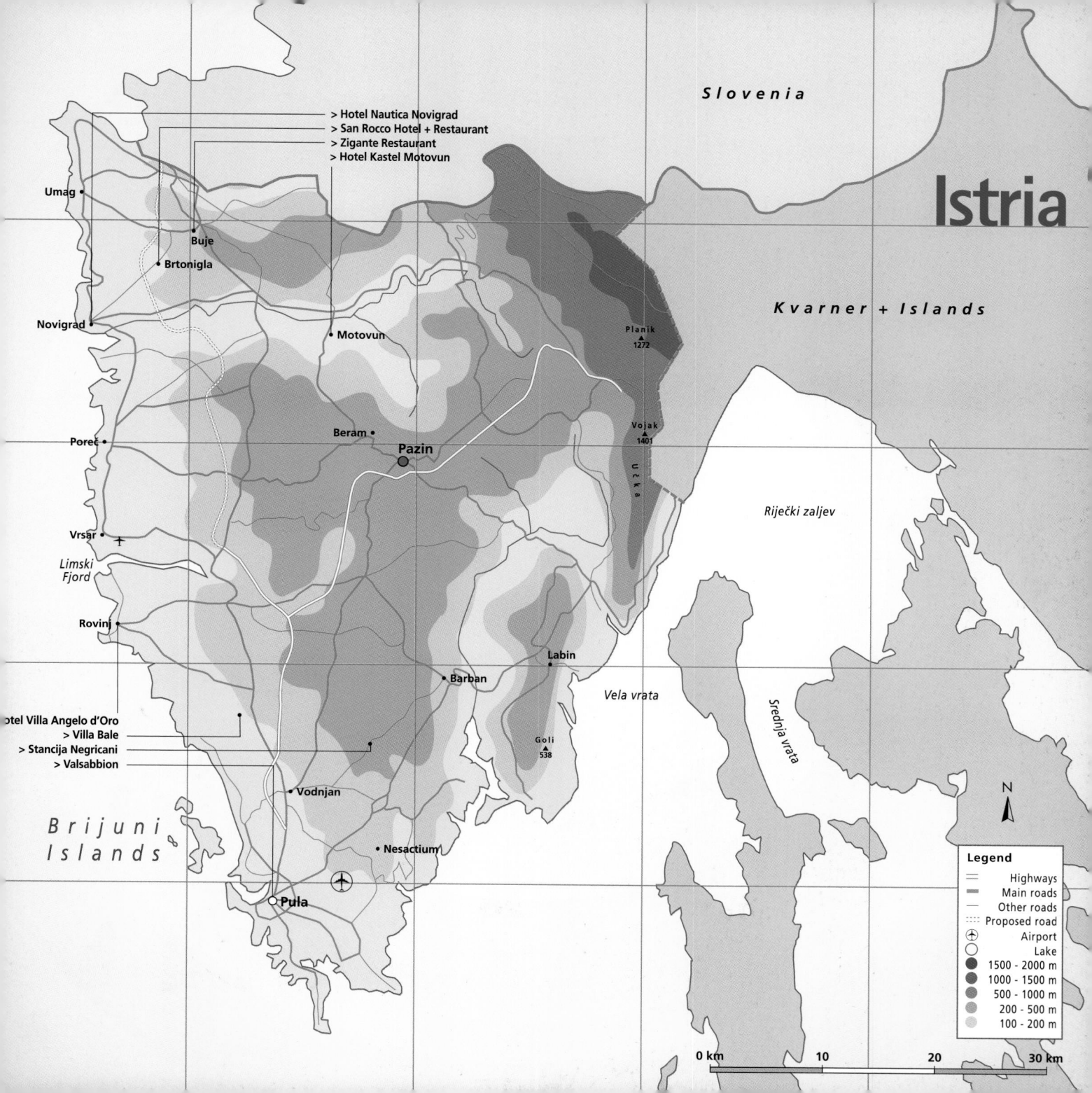

Istria

Slovenia

Kvarner + Islands

> Hotel Nautica Novigrad
> San Rocco Hotel + Restaurant
> Zigante Restaurant
> Hotel Kastel Motovun

Umag

Buje

Brtonigla

Novigrad

Motovun

Poreč

Beram

Pazin

Planik
▲
1272

Vojak
▲
1401

Učka

Riječki zaljev

Vrsar

Limski
Fjord

Rovinj

Labin

Barban

Vela vrata

Goli
538

Srednja vrata

Hotel Villa Angelo d'Oro
> Villa Bale
> Stancija Negricani
> Valsabbion

Vodnjan

Nesactium

N

Brijuni
Islands

Pula

Legend

☰	Highways
▬	Main roads
—	Other roads
┆	Proposed road
✈	Airport
○	Lake
■	1500 - 2000 m
■	1000 - 1500 m
■	500 - 1000 m
■	200 - 500 m
■	100 - 200 m

0 km   10   20   30 km

another tuscany, la dolce vita

The Istrian peninsula lies at the northern end of the Adriatic Sea, punctuated along its boundaries by three main towns: Labin to the east, bordering the Kvarner region; Pula at its southernmost tip; and Umag out west towards the Slovenian frontier, with Trieste, the gateway to Italy, just beyond it.

A golden triangle, steeped in history, Istria has ample evidence of its colourful past: the Histri in prehistoric times, followed by the Romans, the Byzantines, the Venetians and the Austro-Hungarians. Istria combines the grandeur of Rome with the splendour of Byzantium and the refinement of Venice. Istria definitely has an Italian feel to it—not surprising after 400 years of Venetian occupation—with charmingly quaint villages bedecked with vivid rows of colourful washing strung up across narrow streets, lively cafés and countryside full of vineyards, olive groves and cypress trees.

The etymological origins of the word Istria arise from the ancient Greek legend of Jason and the Argonauts, whose name for the Danube was Istros. They thought that the blue river had several mouths, one of them being that of the river Mirna, which they took in order to reach the Adriatic Sea. Later on, in the 3rd century BCE, the incoming Roman conquerors named the peninsula's inhabitants Histri.

As early as the Bronze Age, these indigenous tribal peoples lived in their strong little communities. Mostly hunters, fishermen and shepherds, the Histri took refuge in the hills, in fortified villages surrounded by drystone walls. They lived in low circular huts with flat stone roofs known as 'hiza', still found in the Istrian countryside today.

One such site, Nesactium, thought to have been the Histri's last capital, lies 10 km (6 miles) east of the town of Pula. In 177 BCE, at the time of the Emperor Augustus, the Roman historian Livy wrote an account of the Roman siege of Nesactium. Of immense archeological and cultural importance, the site contains traces of a prehistoric cemetery, Roman thermae and temples, and the foundations of an Early Christian basilica.

PAGE 48: The vast amphitheatre dazzles in the midday sun, a fitting symbol of Roman Pula.

OPPOSITE: The magnificent carved stone Arch of the Sergii forms the great entrance to old Pula.

THIS PAGE (FROM TOP): In the Istrian countryside, the traditional huts were refuges for the peasants; in Groznjan, known as the land of vineyards, cafés (konoba) and hostels are not hard to find.

THIS PAGE: *The Temple of Augustus majestically dominates the main square of Pula. These medieval paving stones are the uppermost layer of an accumulated history that dates back to antiquity.*

OPPOSITE: *The glorious ruins of the amphitheatre are all that are left of the glorious imperial crown that once graced the city of Pula.*

pula, paved with history

The colony of Pola or Pula, the 'Colonia Pulia Pollentia Herculanea' of the Romans, owed its continuing prosperity to roaring maritime trade. Highly coveted by the other empires for its strategic position, it was seized by Byzantium in 539. In 1145, Pula swore allegiance to the Queen of the Adriatic, Venice, its overlord for the next 650 years, until the precipitate arrival of the French in 1797. Then, in 1813, under the Austro-Hungarians, it became the Empire's foremost shipyard. It was subsequently annexed by Italy in 1918, until, in 1947, it became part of the Socialist Federal Republic of Yugoslavia, as the administrative capital of the Croatian province of Istria.

According to the ancient legends, it was the Argonauts who first founded Pula as a temporary settlement while waiting to get their hands on the Golden Fleece before sailing back home to their native Colchis in triumph with the precious trophy.

Pula's golden age was under the Romans, from 43 CE until the fall of the Roman Empire in the 5th century, during which it was an important administrative hub and also a commercial centre. Endowed with the very latest amenities of the time and an impressively advanced infrastructure—baths, sewers, drainage and so on—the city also raised numerous monuments, the ruined remains of which can still be seen today. Other remains are buried deep under the town's medieval paving stones and are just waiting to be discovered and finally brought to light. An ongoing archeological dig is currently underway in Forum Square to unveil the plan of the ancient Roman city.

These ruins have influenced many a writer. The Italian vernacular poet Dante Alighieri, when first passing through Pula, found inspiration in these Roman burial places for his depictions of the terrible 13th-century plague in the ninth circle of the *Inferno* cantica in his epic *Divina Commedia*. In a fairly different vein, author Jules Verne painted a highly detailed picture of the antique ruins of Pula in his serialised novel *Mathias Sandorf*.

Sitting at the southernmost tip of Istria, beside the Adriatic Sea, Pula still appears to be the peninsula's maritime guardian. Nowadays, visitors can see the two faces of Pula: of a city frozen in its glorious past, and of another, more forward-looking city dedicated

These ruins have inspired many a writer.

to its shipbuilding industry. Past and present sometimes mingle. In the city centre, one can take in the extraordinary sight of a quay lined with tall metal cranes and the rusting prow of a merchant ship seemingly wedged between two old buildings.

The road leading into Pula from Rovinj can provide a rather disappointing first view of this industrious city, but the ochre hues of the amphitheatre's stone crown rising up triumphantly in the sun soon take one's breath away. Antique Pula emerges in all its glory. Built like a conch shell, Pula is coiled around a fortress. The city's most important treasures lie along the elliptical route of its main thoroughfare, Sergijevaca street, which transports one from Roman times right up to the Austro-Hungarian Empire.

With one's back to the finely sculpted Arch of the Sergii, the Golden Gate, the view down the busy main street humming with people is impressive at any hour. In the shade of a narrow lane, the small Byzantine Church of St Mary of Formosa, built around 566, is proof of the fervour of the early Christians. Its mosaics are proudly conserved in the Archeological Museum.

Near the seafront, the Cathedral's Renaissance façade and 17th-century bell tower are the indication of one of Christianity's oldest sanctuaries. The foundations were built with stones from the Roman amphitheatre, and the high altar rests on an ancient sarcophagus. Further along the path is the town's main square, once the vast forum, which, with the elegant Temple of Augustus, was the heart of the ancient city. A quick turn-around and one comes face to face with the Gothic edifice which now houses the Town Hall, and its Renaissance arcades, added later. The elegant sobriety of the Franciscan monastery and its cloisters

date from the following century. Even further on, the 17th-century citadel, the work of a distinguished French architect, comes into view, and on the hillside, between the Twin Gate and the Gate of Hercules, lies the city's Archeological Museum, of Austrian inspiration, looking out on the entire city from its great height.

The amphitheatre lies beyond the towering ramparts. Constructed during the reigns of Augustus Claudius and Vespasian in the 1st century CE, it was built to hold more than 20,000 spectators. Made using the plentiful local pale stone, it forms a vast ellipse, over a hectare (2.5 acres) in size, with 72 arches on two levels, topped by a crown. Light floods in from all sides and, when illuminated by the setting sun, as the colour changes from gold to bronze, it stands out as a beacon of Pula's history.

poreč, a small town packed with treasures

Far to the western reaches of Istria, the town of Poreč lies on a peninsula and, from 1902 to 1935, was linked to Parenzana by a small railway line. First founded by the Romans in 129 BCE as a military camp, it had grown into a 'municipium' known as Colonia Julia Parentium by the 1st century CE. The old town still retains the original cruciform street layout from those olden times, with a long central road, the 'decumanus', lying at right angles to another main road, the 'cardo maximus', off which run endless

OPPOSITE: The Basilica of St Mary of Formosa dates back to the Paleochristian era, to the early days of Christianity in Croatia.

THIS PAGE: On the westernmost point of Croatia's Adriatic coastline is the port of Poreč, a haven for pleasure boats, and a stopover by no means to be missed.

narrow lanes. These streets are lined with light-coloured paving stones polished smooth with age, their medieval houses and Gothic and Renaissance palaces still exuding an air of prosperity tempered by the solemnity of antiquity.

Having wandered through the intricate maze of narrow lanes overflowing with souvenir shops whose bright signs mask gracefully ornate façades, and made one's way across Marafor Square with all its knick-knacks and gaudy parasols, down past the canons' house, an unexpected splendour comes into view, at the end of a discreet and inconspicuous passage.

The Basilica of Euphrasius, together with its baptistry and bell tower, is altogether exquisite and, not surprisingly, classified as a UNESCO World Heritage Site. The majority of Poreč's population had converted to Christianity towards the end of the 1st century CE. However, the town's bishop, St Maurus, was martyred during the reign of the Emperor Diocletian, and it was only after the conversion of Emperor Constantine himself, in the 4th century, that Christians were able to practise their religion more openly. The Basilica was constructed between 539 and 553 by Bishop Euphrasius, and is a remarkable synthesis of Roman architecture and Byzantine art. Splendid mosaics fill the apse, glittering with gold, colourfully outlined figures representing popular themes from the New Testament: Christ in Majesty, the Virgin and Child, and the Annunciation. Saints, angels and Bishop Euphrasius himself, carrying a model of the basilica, are depicted all along the apse in a state of beatific grace.

the brijuni islands

The Brijuni archipelago, consisting of 14 distinct islands, now forms a protected marine national park. In the 1st century BCE, the Greek geographer, Strabon, mentioned these islets scattered about the bay of Pula. According to Pliny the Elder, the earliest documents on the subject that can be verified refer to the Insulae Pullariae, the islands of crows, most probably due to the moorhens which used to nest there in great numbers.

OPPOSITE (FROM LEFT): The Basilica's bell tower against the cobalt sky; the grand Basilica of Euphrasius, with its golden cupola, is chief among the city's great treasures.

THIS PAGE: In the cool of Poreč's narrow streets, the paving stones are worn grey and smooth by inexorable time and traffic.

The jewel in the crown is Veli Brijuni, the largest of these islands, where Venus is said to have been born and where Tito built his residence. This, and Mali Brijuni, are the only islands open to visitors, the others are almost untouched. A 10-minute crossing by boat-taxi from the port of Fazana is all that is needed to reach Veli Brijuni.

The blue sea, warm gentle climate and azure light soon won over the Romans who adopted the island as a favourite leisure spot. Overlooking Verige Bay, in a peaceful, verdant spot surrounded by lush cypresses, lie the ruins of a huge and undoubtedly very rich Roman villa, running down to the sea. It is in this enchanted bay that Venus is said to have arisen from a wave and where a temple dedicated to love was consecrated to her.

In more recent times, Communist leader Tito resided on Veli Brijuni and created a safari park which he filled with exotic animals, many of which, like the elephant and the

THIS PAGE (FROM TOP): The beautiful Brijuni islands, dark green jewels scattered across the Adriatic Sea; the remains of a Roman villa on Veli Brijuni, the island being one of the favourite leisure spots for local Roman patrician families.

OPPOSITE: All but an island, but not quite, Rovinj is among the most charming towns along the magnificent Adriatic coastline.

parrot, outlived him. His residence, the White Villa, is not open to visitors, but it was there that he received many distinguished diplomatic guests and where, on 19 July 1965, the Non-Aligned Movement Pact was signed in the presence of Nasser and Nehru.

The route taken to visit the island on foot or on bike does not stray far from the beaten circuit taken by the official tourist train, but is nevertheless a real delight. One may well encounter a herd of red deer huddled in the shade of an oak tree, or a couple of antelope crossing a wooded path. The island is full of laurels, myrtle, magnolias, eucalypti and centuries-old olive trees, all nursed with the utmost love and care—an arboretum with over 3,000 oaks and Aleppo pines, numerous native plant species and over 86 types of exotic plants, as well as the Rose of Brijuni.

rovinj, originally an island

The small town of Rovinj exudes charm, with its red, brick and saffron-coloured rooftops cascading down the hillside, the steeple of St Euphemia's Cathedral grandly rising above it to rival that of San Marco in Venice. Saint and martyr, it is said that her bones miraculously floated into Rovinj in a marble sarcophagus

The very image of a picture postcard...

in 800 BCE. This very same marble sarcophagus of the town's patron saint is proudly ensconced in the church, an object of great devotion.

In the Middle Ages, separated from the mainland by a channel, Rovinj was an island encircled by ramparts with seven soaring gateways. Although now connected to the mainland, the town still has boats moored at its feet,

and tall medieval houses with lines of bright washing hanging between their balconies overlooking the narrow streets, with weathered café tables stacked up on the hillside. The very picture postcard of a rustic island getaway, Rovinj is the perfect place for spending a few lazy days away from the hectic travel schedule.

the istrian interior

After the rugged alpine landscapes of the Kvarner region, the interiors of the Istrian peninsula seem very much softer. Midway between sea and hills, there is plenty of space, valleys widen and cultivated fields alternate with olive groves and terraced vineyards. Even though vertiginously giddy breaches open up in the earth here and there, and perched villages, festooned with cypresses, persist in clinging precariously to rocky promontories, there is an almost Tuscan gentleness to the landscape.

The roads twist and wind away from the shore as they wend their way towards the interior. They rise and descend, devouring hillsides, threading their way through woods before sometimes emerging, miraculously, in a fortified hilltop village.

OPPOSITE: Rovinj is crowned by St Euphemia's Cathedral's steeple.

THIS PAGE (FROM TOP): The Balbi Arch is the gateway leading from the lower reaches of the town to the upper town section; all towns have their fountains, and Rovinj is no exception.

pazin, at the heart of istria

For a long time, this 10th-century fortress situated on a plateau high above the river Pazin was the strategic point of Austria's Istrian territory, the last stronghold against Venetian and Turkish invaders. Rebuilt mostly in the 18th century, the castle houses an ethnographic museum. The writer Jules Verne had his hero Mathias Sandorf, intrepid explorer of the Mediterranean, escape from a keep modelled on it. Although the author never set foot in Pazin, the town pays homage to him in an annual summer festival.

sacred art in beram

Near Beram, in the depths of the countryside, the frescoes in the chapel of St Mary of Skriljinah are considered to be among the most moving and interesting examples of Croatian religious art. They were painted al fresco in 1474 by the local art master Vincent od Kastav in a naïve Renaissance style. Highly colourful and personalised interpretations of key scenes from the Bible and the lives of Jesus Christ, the Virgin Mary and the saints cover the walls right up to the ceiling. Rather less divine in its inspiration is the famous fresco depicting the infernal Dance of Death, which is particularly striking for its realism.

Many of Istria's other religious sites with fresco cycles, such as Vizinada, Zminj and Draguc, are frequently closed. However, the good news is that the keyholder usually lives in the nearest village. Hum is the name of the smallest such site—it takes barely a quarter of an hour to visit.

vineyards and olive groves

'In vino veritas'—the virtues of this Croatian nectar were well-known to Greek navigators way back in ancient times. The lengthy trail of amphorae found at the bottom of the Adriatic is proof of the scale and profitability of this wine trade. The bay of Kalavojna, on the east coast of Istria, comes from the Greek 'kalos oinos' (good wine). Exactly where Vinum Pucinum was grown is not

THIS PAGE (FROM TOP): The Chapel of St Mary of Skriljinah is unique in Croatia, with frescoes of the Last Judgment and Dance of Death; lush vineyards and olive groves flourish side by side in Istria.
OPPOSITE: The view from Motovun is nothing short of spectacular.

...the virtues of Croatian nectar were known to Greek navigators way back in ancient times.

known. The hills of Sovinjak Buzet and Motovun both claim this honour. More certain, however, is that this local wine was very much prized by Emperor Julius Augustus, who attributed his long life to its virtues. In the Middle Ages, Muscat from Istria was served at royal tables, and the Republic of Venice, during its occupation of the region, granted itself the lucrative monopoly on wine. Under the Austro-Hungarian Empire, 3,000 hectares (7,413 acres) of vines were planted in Istria. Today, wine is booming business for Istria. Little known beyond its own shores, tourists can discover and savour it at their leisure. There are about a hundred commercial winegrowers in Istria, and many of them are open to the public for winetasting and buying. The most commonly grown grape variety is the Malvasia, which produces a refreshing dry white wine, straw-yellow in colour, with a bouquet of white flowers, drunk with seafood, white meat and truffles. Momjan Muscat and Pink Muscat from the Poreč region are delicately sweet and light, being the perfect accompaniment to desserts. Teran has a stronger flavour and robust character, a deep ruby red, tasting of wild berries and perfect for game and other dark meat. When it is still young, it is a common ingredient used in the highly popular bread soup.

Wine grapes and olive trees share the same growing conditions—similar soil and exposure—and are particularly concentrated in the northern part of Istria, between the Mirna river and the Slovenian border. Four official wine circuits have been created, in close collaboration with 93 winegrowers and vineyard owners, in the areas around Rovinj, from Vodnjan to Poreč, Buje or Pazin. Maps are readily available from all the tourist offices. There is also an olive oil circuit definitely worth exploring.

istria's black gold

It all began in 1929, when some Italian workmen who were constructing the railway line between Trieste and Istria happened to unearth some truffles in the Mirna valley. These fungi were subsequently sold in Italy under the Alba appellation.

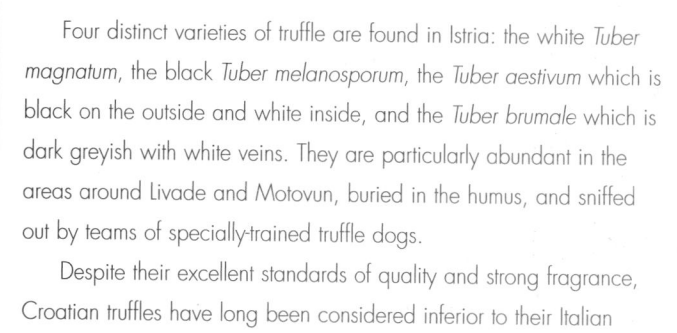

Four distinct varieties of truffle are found in Istria: the white *Tuber magnatum*, the black *Tuber melanosporum*, the *Tuber aestivum* which is black on the outside and white inside, and the *Tuber brumale* which is dark greyish with white veins. They are particularly abundant in the areas around Livade and Motovun, buried in the humus, and sniffed out by teams of specially-trained truffle dogs.

Despite their excellent standards of quality and strong fragrance, Croatian truffles have long been considered inferior to their Italian rival. However, in 1999 the first step was taken towards creating a much-deserved reputation for them. On 2 November 1999, Giancarlo Zigante, a local inhabitant out walking his pet dog, discovered the largest known *Tuber*, weighing in at 1.3 kg (3 lb), which immediately made it into the Guinness Book of Records. Zigante had a bronze cast made of his truffle and then served it up at a memorable feast he hosted for a hundred people in order to promote Istrian truffles. It made headlines in all the local and national newspapers, and led to Croatian truffles acquiring official recognition.

Zigante wasted no time in taking full advantage of his country's new star. He opened a specialist truffle restaurant called Zigante Restaurant in the small town of Livade, near Motovun, itself the new truffle centre. Truffles are now found on the menus of all the local restaurants, typically served with pasta, risotto, polenta or potatoes. More adventurous recipes include it with wild asparagus and mushrooms, both of which grow abundantly in the region. In his own restaurant, Zigante dreams up skilful combinations such as truffles with white chocolate or sorbets. Livade has a truffle festival for several days in October, to coincide with truffle harvest time, while Motovun has its turn over the third weekend in October.

OPPOSITE (FROM TOP): Enjoy an open-air meal in the great outdoors, surrounded by the vineyards and olive groves of Istria's countryside; a fresh herb salad and wild asparagus risotto accompanied by some great cheese make a hearty Croatian repast, with a gourmet touch of truffle shavings.

THIS PAGE (FROM TOP): The delicate flavours of fresh seafood are subtly complemented by truffles; pigs have a very keen sense for truffles but must be supervised lest they eat up the delicacies.

agrotourism on the rise

Green tourism existed long before the term was invented. For years, more adventurous travellers have ventured into Istria's verdant hinterland. Happy to escape the large spa-hotels and crowded camping sites on the coast, they headed inland to explore the countryside on foot or bicycle. They preferred to stay with locals en route in order to experience the richness of genuine rural hospitality and got to know the real Istria.

Helping out in the fields, having a go at milking the cows, hunting for berries and mushrooms, participating in a local feast or taking part in the grape harvest were all seen as part and parcel of the fun. Staying in people's houses as if guests, sharing in their daily tasks and most especially savouring proper home-cooking were the very real pleasures for these first adventurers whom the locals viewed affectionately as eccentrics with a penchant for the smell of fresh bread, hay and goat's cheese.

As new notions of ecology and nature conservation began to take root, this taste for experiencing the Croatian countryside led to the development of agrotourism, which sets standards for accommodation and organised outdoor activities. Not only does this involve the whole community and its way of life, but also the indigenous industries of hunting, fishing, local crafts, customs and regional products, in order to promote the high quality of hospitality which today's sophisticated travellers now expect.

Today, there's no end to the number of paths and circuits open to hikers, cyclists or others in search of pastoral or cultural enrichment. Whether village houses for rent, hotels in family homes, stays in viticultural properties or working farms, private villas or simple bed and breakfasts, the choice is vast, depending on one's taste and budget. All of them are listed out in a useful multilingual guide available from all the various tourist offices in the region.

THIS PAGE (FROM TOP): A Tuscan sky illuminates an Istrian landscape; traditional fishing methods are still used in Istria every day.

OPPOSITE: With the increasing demand for agrotourism, non-polluting outdoor activities such as hiking and cycling on marked trails are quickly developing.

PAGE 68 AND 69: The magnificent ruin of a medieval castle at Ovigrad is still awaiting the return of its questing knights.

...this taste for the countryside led to the development of 'agrotourism'...

San Rocco Hotel + Restaurant

THIS PAGE (FROM TOP): *The Restaurant San Rocco serves local cuisine; the pool terrace where hotel guests can enjoy their meals.*

OPPOSITE (CLOCKWISE FROM LEFT): *Exposed wooden beams lend a rustic air to the cosy bedroom; the welcoming hotel lobby; guests can relax at the wine bar for a post-prandial drink.*

The small hilltop town of Brtonigla lies near the Adriatic some 30 km (18.6 miles) from the border with Italy. It was first settled during the Bronze Age, and several ancient ruins remain from that period. Fortifications left from the Roman conquest gave way to a series of feudal castles, which led to the development of the town as it is today.

At the heart of the town is the San Rocco Hotel and Restaurant. This intimate, family-owned and -run boutique hotel consists of three lovingly restored farm buildings, all

beautifully furnished and decorated. The first of these contains most of the hotel's 12 bedrooms. Each of these has been individually and sympathetically styled, with some offering a sea view and others overlooking the town itself. Exposed walls, beamed ceilings and wooden floors are common features. All rooms come fully equipped with air-conditioning, mini-bar, satellite television, safe, and Internet connections. Several also have special facilities for the disabled.

This building also contains a cosy wine bar, and the hotel's gourmet restaurant that prides itself on being one of the finest in the region. Dishes include seasonal specialities typical to Istria, such as locally sourced truffles, mushrooms, and air-dried ham and game, which can all be accompanied by Istrian wines such as Malvasia and Terrano from San Rocco's substantial wine cellar.

Meals, including breakfast, can also be served on a terrace overlooking the garden and an attractive outdoor pool.

The second building is a function room suitable for a range of social events, and also houses the wine cellar. The third building consists of an open terrace and wellness centre that comes with a pool, sauna and massage facilities where guests can enjoy some well-deserved pampering.

The pristine surrounding land is well known for its vineyards, which produce the region's acclaimed Malvasia and Terrano wines. It also offers plenty of opportunities for outdoor enthusiasts, with hiking, horse riding, cycling and other activities all readily available. And Brtonigla itself is famous for its konobas (local family-run restaurants) and wine cellars where the region's wines are produced and can be tasted.

FACTS

ROOMS	12 rooms
FOOD	Restaurant San Rocco: Istrian
DRINK	wine bar
FEATURES	wellness centre • facilities for the disabled • dog kennels
BUSINESS	meeting room
NEARBY	Brtonigla • Adriatic coast
CONTACT	Srednja Ulica 2, 52474 Brtonigla • telephone: +385.52.725 000 • facsimile: +385.52.725 026 • email: info@san-rocco.hr • website: www.san-rocco.hr

PHOTOGRAPHS COURTESY OF SAN ROCCO HOTEL + RESTAURANT.

Hotel Nautica Novigrad

Until recently, the Adriatic coastline of Croatia was one of Europe's best-kept secrets, known only to a handful of intrepid visitors. Ever since the country opened up at the end of the last century, however, that secret has got out and now the area is one of Europe's most talked about destinations.

With its calm, clear azure waters, Mediterranean climate, historic towns and friendly people, Croatia's coastline more than deserves its new status as a tourist hotspot. More importantly, it has adapted rapidly to ensure that visitors enjoy the service and quality other more established destinations have long offered.

One fine example of this development is the Hotel Nautica Novigrad on the Istrian peninsula. Located on the seafront just outside of the 1,400-year-old town, this brand new luxury resort has been built around a beautiful marina on a naturally deep and sheltered cove in Novigrad bay. With 365 sea and 50 dry berths, as well as room for mega-yachts, the marina provides all the services and facilities that the seagoing traveller could want, including a service centre, fuel station, laundry, changing and washing facilities—even a dental surgery!

The attached hotel maintains this nautical theme in both its design and character, which evoke the glorious ocean-going liners of old. One of the most luxurious on the Adriatic, it boasts 38 designer rooms

THIS PAGE (FROM TOP): Tranquillity permeates the elegant interior of the hotel's wellness centre; stunning views of the marina can be slowly enjoyed at leisure after an afternoon of activity.

OPPOSITE (FROM LEFT): An exquisite dining experience awaits at the acclaimed Navigare Restaurant; soothing colours and nautical themes define each one of the luxurious rooms in the hotel.

and four lavishly furnished apartments, all of which come with the latest technology and superb views of the sea or nearby town.

The hotel prides itself on having a first-class à la carte restaurant. Using carefully selected and locally sourced ingredients, the Navigare Restaurant specialises in Istrian dishes such as truffles, asparagus and wind-dried ham. The lounge bar and state-of-the-

art conference centre make the hotel perfect for events ranging from business meetings to wedding receptions.

For those seeking a little mental and physical regeneration during their visit, the resort has a wellness centre that incorporates indoor pool, children's pool, Turkish bath, Finnish sauna, aroma showers, and fully equipped fitness studio. There is also a

beauty salon that offers a variety of massages and numerous other facial and body treatments to relax and recharge.

The nearby town of Novigrad is ideal for those hours spent outside the resort. With its charming layout and old stone buildings, this historic centre reflects the various cultural influences that have shaped Croatia's history. A great way to end the day is to take a leisurely walk through the streets enjoying all the sights from eighth-century fortifications and old towers to magnificent Renaissance palaces and medieval churches.

FACTS		
ROOMS	38 rooms • 4 suites	
FOOD	Navigare Restaurant: Istrian	
DRINK	Nautica Lounge Bar	
FEATURES	wellness centre • beauty salon • pool • tennis courts • children's playground • dental clinic	
BUSINESS	meeting room	
NEARBY	Venice • Trieste • Pula • Porec	
CONTACT	Sv Antona 15, 52466 Novigrad • telephone: +385.52.600 400 • facsimile: +385.52.600 450 • email: info@nauticahotels.com • website: www.nauticahotels.com	

PHOTOGRAPHS COURTESY OF HOTEL NAUTICA NOVIGRAD.

Hotel Kastel Motovun

When the world finally realised Croatia's potential as a first-class tourist destination in the 1990s, it was the coast that attracted the majority—if not all—of the attention. The belated accolades the beautiful and unspoilt coastline drew were fully justified, but sadly overlooked the country's enchanting interior. This 'other Croatia' boasts some of the most dramatic and best-preserved medieval towns in existence, one of which is the little mountaintop town of Motovun, right at the heart of the Istrian peninsula.

Legend has it that the town was built by giants living in the valleys below, but its true origins are more likely to lie in the Middle Ages when marauding bandits forced local inhabitants to fortify their hilltop settlement. Motovun commands extensive views of the surrounding pristine countryside, setting off the town's rich architectural and cultural heritage and making it a truly memorable holiday destination for all.

Today, this small town retains much of its original character and the features for which it became famous, including a Venetian-era square, ancient churches, medieval city walls, and a street layout that has remained unchanged for almost a thousand years. The

THIS PAGE (FROM TOP): **The hotel's cheery red façade warmly reflects the atmosphere within; a cosy and softly lit guestroom; the hilltop location ensures splendid views for miles.**

OPPOSITE (FROM LEFT): **The hotel's restaurant offers unique local cuisine and Istrian wines; the carefully maintained grounds are a distinct pleasure to walk in.**

Romanesque, Mediterranean and Germanic culinary traditions. Delicacies unique to the area include wind-dried Istrian ham, a local variation of minestrone and local black and white varieties of the highly prized truffles.

The hotel's central location allows guests to enjoy the town's attractions, and serves as a base for exploring the surrounding area. The nearby historical towns of Pazin, Beram,

Hum, Poreč and Rovinj are all within easy driving distance. Slightly further afield at the southern end of the Istrian peninsula is the cultural hub of Pula, as is the beautiful group of islands which comprise the Brijuni National Park. Outdoor sports enthusiasts will also be spoilt for choice, as horse riding, canoeing, hiking, bike tours and hunting are all easily arranged.

town's only hotel, the Hotel Kastel Motovun, reflects this attachment to history. This former castle overlooking the main square has been recently renovated and is now a family-owned and family-run concern offering 28 rooms, all with clear views of the town and surrounding landscape.

In addition, the hotel boasts a cheerful little café, an art gallery and one of the best restaurants in the region, the newly renovated Blue Dining Room. It serves à la carte meals reflecting the many influences predominant in Croatia, including Slavic,

FACTS		
ROOMS	28 rooms • 2 suites • 1 apartment
FOOD	Blue Dining Room: local
DRINK	Istrian wines • hotel café
FEATURES	art gallery • massage room
BUSINESS	meeting rooms • Internet connection
NEARBY	Motovun • Pazin • Beram • Hum • Poreč • Rovinj
CONTACT	Trg Andrea Antico 7, 52424 Motovun • telephone: +385.52.681 607 • facsimile: +385.52.681 652 • email: info@hotel-kastel-motovun.hr • website: www.hotel-kastel-motovun.hr

PHOTOGRAPHS COURTESY OF HOTEL KASTEL MOTOVUN.

Hotel Villa Angelo d'Oro

Situated on a hill almost completely surrounded by the sea and only connected to the mainland by a narrow isthmus, the town of Rovinj on the Istrian peninsula can date its existence back to prehistoric times. It was colonised by the Romans and the town continued to expand until the late Middle Ages, at which point the inhabitants simply ran out of room and as a consequence all further development seems to have come to a halt. An unforeseen but charming result of this is that even today Rovinj retains all of the medieval character and charm with which it was originally imbued—much in the same way that its neighbour Venice has, but with winding cobbled streets instead of canals.

Located on one of the most beautiful streets at the heart of this pedestrian town is the Hotel Villa Angelo d'Oro, a 17th-century former bishop's palace that has been lovingly restored in recent times to its original medieval splendour. This cosily intimate and charming venue, furnished in exquisite taste with period furniture and carefully selected oil paintings throughout, has 24 delightful rooms and suites and offers an ideal place to stay on any visit to the town.

Although there are many restaurants to be found in the surrounding streets and alleyways, guests need not look any further than the Villa Angelo d'Oro's own restaurant for a top-notch dining experience. The hotel's restaurant menu offers the finest international gourmet cuisine, all served right under the watchful eye of the famous golden angel for which the hotel is named. Noted specialities here include fish and seafood caught by local fishermen, as well as expertly prepared

THIS PAGE (FROM TOP): A charming guestroom decorated in soft swathes of turquoise and teal; the Restaurant Angelo d'Oro with its eponymous angel statue; the elegant yet relaxed lounge.

OPPOSITE (FROM LEFT): Guests can enjoy relaxing in the hotel garden terrace, where light refreshments are served all day; the Hotel Villa Angelo d'Oro is scattered about with various secluded comfortable nooks, each a pleasure to discover.

...one of the most beautiful and unspoilt stretches of coastline in Europe.

Mediterranean vegetation and helpful staff help to create a protective oasis of peace and quiet. Alternatively, the hotel will be pleased to arrange boat trips to the many islands of the Rovinj Archipelago that lie just offshore, enabling visitors to enjoy the clear waters, empty beaches and secluded coves of one of the most beautiful and unspoilt stretches of coastline in Europe.

Mediterranean dishes and local delicacies such as Istrian ham and cheese. Wines can be selected directly from the hotel's extensive wine cellar, and a glass of grappa is the perfect way to round off any meal.

Having enjoyed the hustle and bustle of a day in the town, guests are invited to slow down, relax and enjoy the more serene atmosphere the hotel has to offer. For those so inclined, such sanctuary can be found in the library on the top floor where the former bishop's favourite terrace offers wonderful unobstructed views over nearby rooftops, clear through to the lovely Bay of Rovinj and beyond. For others, there's the spa centre with its Finnish sauna, Turkish bath, jacuzzi, tanning beds and massage parlour. Lastly, there's the hotel garden where the lush

FACTS		
	ROOMS	24 rooms
	FOOD	Restaurant Angelo d'Oro: international
	DRINKS	Garden Bar • wine cellar
	FEATURES	spa • private parking • motorboat facilities
	NEARBY	Rovinj • Rovinj Archipelago • coastal bathing beaches
	CONTACT	Via Svalba 38-42, 52210 Rovinj • telephone: +385.52.840 502 • facsimile: +385.52.840 112 • email: hotel.angelo@vip.hr • website: www.angelodoro.hr

PHOTOGRAPHS COURTESY OF HOTEL VILLA ANGELO D'ORO.

Villa Bale

As a general rule, it's a good idea to consult an expert before buying or renting something for the first time, and this is as true for holiday villas as it is for anything else. An expert can sift through the properties on offer and select the best one suited to specific tastes. He knows local nuances and ways of doing business, preventing embarrassing mistakes or misunderstandings. He has the advantage of having worked with particular property owners before, thereby lessening the chance of any last-minute hitches. An expert, in short, increases the likelihood that the holiday is a success and not a failure.

With this in mind, anyone choosing to book a holiday villa would be well advised to approach The Villa Book, an agency created by some of the most knowledgeable people in the business. With over 25 years of experience, they pride themselves on long, close working relationships with property owners and agents. As a result, they are able to pinpoint and address an individual client's preferences, right down to the size and style of property, its location, and any special services required, such as babysitters or yacht charters.

The Villa Book offers hundreds of properties over three continents, but they are particularly strong on villas in and around the Mediterranean and Adriatic seas. Croatia is one such major tourist hotspot where they are well represented, and one of their finest properties in the country is Villa

THIS PAGE (FROM TOP): **The sweeping panorama of unspoilt country vistas from the Villa Bale; a vine-covered pergola shelters the open dining area on the terrace outside the main house.**

OPPOSITE (CLOCKWISE FROM LEFT): **The interiors possess traditional features such as wooden beams, stone floors and fireplaces; rooms are dressed in warm hues; homely touches and knick-knacks complete the look.**

Bale, situated in a quiet rural location just inland of the Adriatic Coast on the beautiful and pristine Istrian peninsula.

Set in private grounds, and surrounded by woods, fields and vineyards, the property comprises a century-old stone farmhouse and annex. In the last few years, these buildings have been lovingly restored to the very highest standards, so that they now have all the modern amenities expected of one of The Villa Book's properties, without having lost any of their unique character.

The garden consists of a large flat lawn dotted with mature trees. This also contains two pools—one indoor, one outdoor, to suit all weather conditions. There are a total of four double bedrooms that, together with the spacious reception rooms, retain many traditional features, including beamed ceilings, their original floors and large fireplaces. There is also a well equipped gym and sauna, and bicycles are also available for those who might wish to explore the beautiful countryside.

FACTS		
	ROOMS	4 double rooms
	FOOD	full-time cook
	DRINK	welcome wine pack • espresso coffee maker
	FEATURES	indoor pool • outdoor pool • sauna • bicycles
	NEARBY	Betiga • Rovinj • Pula • Adriatic Sea
	CONTACT	12 Venetian House, 47 Warrington Crescent, London W9 1EJ • telephone: +44.845.500 2000 • facsimile: +44.845.500 2001 • email: info@thevillabook.com • website: www.thevillabook.com

PHOTOGRAPHS COURTESY OF THE VILLA BOOK.

Stancija Negricani

The Istrian peninsula in western Croatia is a verdant land set against the rippling azure of the Adriatic, and at its tranquil heart is the lovingly restored farmhouse hotel, Stancija Negricani. Located 6 km (4 miles) north of the medieval town of Vodnjan, the hotel is within easy reach of the town's various historical and cultural attractions. This scenic region is ideal for those seeking a glimpse of Croatia's traditional country lifestyle, and the Stancija Negricani hotel is an excellent point from which to begin a thorough exploration of the surrounding area.

The welcoming Modrusan family runs this charming hotel as one might a home. The affable and indulgent Mario-Jumbo and Mirjana positively encourage midnight raids on the kitchen. Stomachs tend not to grumble after hours, however, with generous portions of old-fashioned Istrian home-cooking with freshly baked bread served at each meal.

Over the years, countless guests have experienced countryside Croatia at its best, and the hotel's bloom-filled terraces are ideal spots in which to appreciate its delights, being open to the weather and scents blown in by the breeze from the herb garden. The hotel's endearing guestrooms are named for wild medicinal and aromatic herbs that grow here, Divlja Ruza (wild rose) to Vinova loza (grapevine) being two examples of this quaint practice. Each room is decorated in a tasteful old-fashioned way, reminiscent of a previous generation's attention to intricate detail and craftsmanship. The wooden beds have sturdy, hand-carved, roll-top frames, the

THIS PAGE (FROM TOP): The Stancija Negricani farmhouse hotel has been lovingly restored, retaining its original character and look; the rambling old farmhouse and its well-manicured grounds are a sight for travel-weary eyes.

OPPOSITE (CLOCKWISE FROM LEFT): Exposed stone walls and other quaint features are a part of the hotel's charm, a reminder that one is holidaying in the country; flowers in the window bring out the warm atmosphere within; a table temptingly laid out with various delectables in the sun.

...ideal for those seeking a glimpse of Croatia's traditional lifestyle...

antique dressers are all handmade, and the ceiling light fixtures are ornately patterned. The property's renovation has only enhanced its architectural appeal. Aged timber beams are deliberately showcased throughout, and dark wood shutters still frame each window. The walls are sensuously tactile, revealing the original rough-hewn stonework beneath and each doorframe is unique, featuring quirky and creative carpentry before the days of pre-fabricated standardisation.

Stancija Negricani's outdoor and open air spaces are ambrosia for all the senses, redolent with clear views of the countryside stretching out across the Fazana peninsula and Brijuni islands. When town-hopping around this richly diverse region, a stay at the Stancija Negricani should be pencilled in for the warmth of its hosts, the tradition and history that imbue its very walls, and the sheer delight of it all. This is authentic Croatia as it was, is, and should be.

FACTS		
	ROOMS	9 rooms
	FOOD	traditional home-cooked (all meals)
	FEATURES	satellite TV • Internet connection • laptop rental • horseriding • hiking • cycling • outdoor pool • volleyball court
	NEARBY	Pula airport • Vodnjan • Fazana beach resort • horse riding
	CONTACT	Stancija Negricani farmhouse, 52206 Marcana, Stancija Negricani bb • telephone: +385.52.391 084 • facsimile: +385.52.580 840 • email: konoba-jumbo@pu.t-com.hr • website: www.stancijanegricani.com

PHOTOGRAPHS COURTESY OF STANCIJA NEGRICANI.

Valsabbion

The Valsabbion Hotel and Restaurant is in possession of an impressively star-studded guest book, having played host to global celebrities, the likes of which include pop singer Sting, thespian Jeremy Irons, Latin balladeer Julio Iglesias and supermodel Naomi Campbell. A small yet stylish boutique hotel with the air of an exclusive members' club, the family-owned Valsabbion stands high above a sheltered bay and is the ideal base from which to explore the Mediterranean shores and the rolling, verdant hills of the beautiful Istrian Riviera.

Repeat winner of Istria's Best Restaurant award, the Valsabbion is if nothing else a gastronomic paradise. In 2005 and 2006 it was voted Croatia's Best Restaurant by *Gault Millau*. With sensational seafood and local white truffle dishes a speciality, the executive chef keeps diners returning time after time with inventive menus and inspired culinary creations. The lack of mainstream

buzz from the street has only added to its allure as the place to be for those in the know on the very top of the travel circuit.

Standing out on the restaurant's open-air terrace and relaxing appreciatively in the balmy evening air is an experience best complemented by a perfectly chilled glass of blossom-scented Malvazija (a delicate local white wine), a unique experience glossed by modernity, tempered with warm intimacy, that even the most cosmopolitan traveller will hold comparable to any found in the celebrated style havens of London or Paris.

The Valsabbion has 10 comfortable and tastefully decorated rooms and suites, some of which have private balconies overlooking the nearby harbour. The design of these generously proportioned modern

living spaces is bold, simple and indicative of a strong sense of style. Rich textures form a lush tactile palette—inviting leather sofas are clad in shades of oxblood, while sleek Zen pieces grace the gleaming surfaces.

The dermatologist-run Wellness Centre has a menu almost as impressive as that of its renowned restaurant. The vast range of

treatments includes manicures, depilation, skin peels, aromatherapy and rejuvenating facials. Nutritional advice involving exercise programmes and hypnosis is also available. Body wraps, warm oil relaxation therapies and chocolate massage are specialities of the house, and those who prefer a higher level of discreet maintenance may choose from a wide selection of cosmetic treatments administered under the watchful eye of a fully qualified in-house professional.

The Valsabbion's art-deco façade stands within sight of the marina and the coast, close enough that the soft beach air breathes through the hotel as naturally as the tide rises on the shore. The historic city of Pula is just minutes away, its amphitheatre, museums and Roman ruins waiting to be explored. In this environment, it is hardly any wonder that the only difficulty guests will likely face during their stay is a wholehearted reluctance to leave at the end.

THIS PAGE: *The Valsabbion's pool with a commanding view of the nearby harbour is located in the wellness centre on the top floor.*

OPPOSITE (CLOCKWISE FROM TOP): *The acclaimed Restaurant Valsabbion serves award-winning cuisine in its relaxed yet elegant settings; all the hotel's stylish guestrooms are wholly conducive to days of pure relaxation and pampering; attention to detail is apparent in each careful touch of furnishing.*

FACTS		
ROOMS	6 double rooms • 3 suites • 1 family room	
FOOD	The Restaurant Valsabbion: seafood	
DRINK	wine list	
FEATURES	satellite TV • wireless Internet connection • safety deposit box • wellness centre • hydrotherapy • massage • solarium • pet-friendly	
NEARBY	golf is available on the Brijuni islands	
CONTACT	Pjescana Uvala IX/26, 52100 Pula • telephone: +385.52.218 033 • facsimile: +385.52.383 333 • email: info@valsabbion.hr • website: www.valsabbion.hr	

PHOTOGRAPHS COURTESY OF VALSABBION.

Zigante Restaurant

The Zigante Restaurant and Truffle Company has a rather unique entry in the *Guinness World Records*. In 1999, its manager Giancarlo Zigante and his trusty dog Diana were walking in an Istrian wood when they discovered the largest truffle in history, weighing in at an astounding 1.3 kg (3 lb). Building on this success, Zigante Truffles expanded its retail section and now has five outlets located throughout Istria.

The village of Livade was the setting for Giancarlo's dramatic discovery. Home to the company's original truffle store, 2002 saw the opening of its highly acclaimed Zigante Restaurant, which specialises in exquisitely fresh truffle dishes prepared by Damir Modrušan, one of Croatia's top five chefs.

This restaurant ascended to the top of Croatia's gastronomic ladder within just two years. Highly rated by culinary bibles such as *Gault Millau*, its sterling efforts were rewarded in 2005 with the coveted title of Restaurant of the Year. Fresh truffles can be enjoyed at Zigante Restaurant year-round. White truffles are available from September until January, while their black counterparts

THIS PAGE: The warmly lit Zigante Restaurant in Livade serves up exquisite truffle dishes based on regional culinary traditions.

OPPOSITE: Zigante Truffles also has five shops and outlets located throughout Istria, where high quality black and white truffles and their products are on sale.

are in season from May until November. Damir and his chefs also love creating dishes showcasing other local specialities such as mushrooms and asparagus.

From the à la carte menu, opt for the simply outstanding Symphony of Truffles. This phenomenal dish is historical and cultural gastronomy, an inspired creation featuring as its main characters the distinguishing representatives of Croatian cuisine: polenta, asparagus, scampi and, of course, truffles. Other popular dishes include the baby beef tagliata or fish carpaccio with truffles, or the delectable gnocchio alla nona with a chocolate and truffle filling. Dessert options for the adventurous include sheep's cheese with honey and truffles or rich, smooth ice cream, with the ubiquitous truffles.

The interior pairs original stonework and exposed wooden beams with sleek and stylishly laid tables. The newly extended restaurant now boasts two dining rooms seating up to 44 guests in an elegant setting, or parties of up to 74. The sheltered terrace can accommodate 60. New additions include an intimate VIP room for exclusive parties, and even special accommodation for diners' treasured pets.

Wine enthusiasts will be pleased to find that the piquant aroma of Zigante's truffles is perfectly accentuated with a fine vintage. Award-winning sommelier Emil Perdec is always on hand to recommend a suitable wine from his list, which features classic wines from Bordeaux, Tuscany and Australia alongside Croatia's most revered names.

Due to their extreme paucity, truffles, white or black, are high on the list of the most extravagantly priced ingredients per pound in the world. One may then relax in the knowledge that Zigante is a keen proponent of the 'Slow Food' movement, wherein the practice of lingering over each course and savouring every bite is actively encouraged. So for an unforgettable Croatian dining experience featuring these 'white diamonds' and 'black pearls' of gastronomy, as they say in the rarefied circles of haute cuisine, follow your nose—all the way to Zigante.

FACTS

FOOD	truffles • local fine dining
FEATURES	2 indoor dining rooms • sheltered terrace • VIP room • pet-friendly
CONTACT	Livade-Levade 7, 52427 Livade-Levade • telephone: +385.52.664 302 • facsimile: +385.52.664 303 • email: restaurantzigante@livadetartufi.com • website: www.zigantetartufi.com

PHOTOGRAPHS COURTESY OF ZIGANTE TRUFFLES AND CROATIAN NATIONAL TOURIST BOARD.

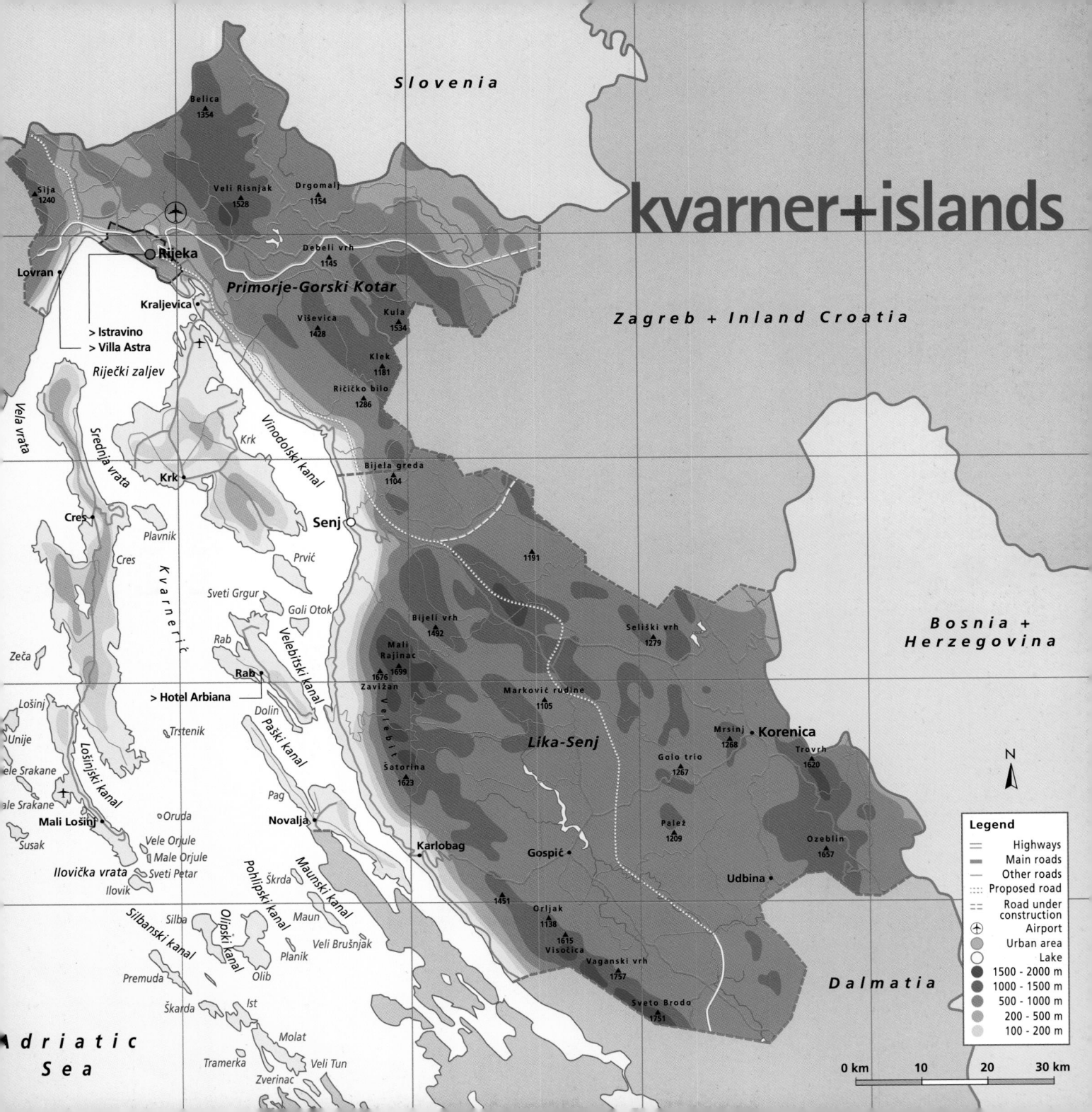

kvarner+islands

Slovenia

▲ Belica
1354

▲ Šija
1240

▲ Veli Risnjak
1528

▲ Drgomalj
1154

✈ **Rijeka** ◉

Lovran ▾

Kraljevica ▲

▲ Debeli vrh
1145

Primorje-Gorski Kotar

> **Istravino**
> **Villa Astra**

Riječki zaljev

▲ Viševica
1428

▲ Kula
1534

▲ Klek
1181

▲ Ričičko bilo
1286

Zagreb + Inland Croatia

Vela vrata

Srednja vrata

Krk

Vinodolski kanal

Krk ▲

▲ Bijela greda
1104

Senj ◯

▲ 1191

Cres ▲

Plavnik

Prvić

Sveti Grgur

Goli Otok

▲ Bijeli vrh
1492

▲ Seliški vrh
1279

Bosnia +
Herzegovina

Cres

Kvarnerić

Rab

Rab

▲ Mali
Rajinac
1676 1699

Zavižan

Marković rudine
▲ 1105

Lika-Senj

Mrsinj ▲ ● **Korenica**
1268

Trovrh
▲ 1620

> **Hotel Arbiana**

Dolin

Paški kanal

Zeča

Lošinj

Unije

Velebitski kanal

Velebit

▲ Šatorina
1623

Golo trio
▲ 1267

Palež
▲ 1209

Ozeblin
▲ 1657

ele Srakane

ale Srakane

Lošinjski kanal

Trstenik

✝

○ Oruda

Vele Orjule

Mali Lošinj ●

Pag

Novalja ▾

Karlobag ●

Gospić ●

Udbina ●

Susak

Male Orjule

Sveti Petar

Ilovička vrata

Ilovik

Škrda

▲ 1451

Orljak
▲ 1138

Maunski kanal

Silbanski kanal

Pohlipski kanal

Maun

Planik

Veli Brušnjak

Visočica
▲ 1615

Vaganski vrh
▲ 1757

N
↑

Premuda

Silba

Olipski kanal

Olib

Ist

Sveto Brodo
▲ 1751

Dalmatia

Adriatic
Sea

Škarda

Molat

Tramerka

Veli Tun

Zverinac

Legend

≡	Highways
▬	Main roads
—	Other roads
⋯	Proposed road
══	Road under construction
✈	Airport
●	Urban area
○	Lake
	1500 - 2000 m
	1000 - 1500 m
	500 - 1000 m
	200 - 500 m
	100 - 200 m

0 km   10   20   30 km

the four corners of heaven

Situated in the northern part of the Adriatic where the Mediterranean penetrates deepest into old Europe, the Kvarner region provides Central Europe with a splendid balcony overlooking the sea. Kvarner derives its name from the Latin, Quarter-narius (the four corners of heaven), the place where the four cardinal points meet, neatly summing up the importance of Kvarner's geographical position.

A haven for tourism, the Gulf of Kvarner is a particularly rich and varied region: a ragged coastline to the north where the mountains meet sea, and the seaside resort of Opatija; numerous islands in the middle; and the wooded summits of Gorski Kotar inland. Immensely popular in the 19th century, it still has plenty to offer tourists today. Lovran, Opatija and Volosko make up a succession of small fishing ports, villages and seaside resorts wedged between the sea and the surrounding hills, which provide an alternative Riviera for visitors. Picturesque and welcoming, these quaint towns bask sleepily in the sun amidst its stunning coastal views and glittery, transparent water.

opatija, a step back in time

Overlooking the gulf, Opatija is a mass of grand palaces and villas, overflowing with architectural wonders from the 19th century in pure Austro-Hungarian style, all the rage in Vienna at the time. Pink-fronted pâtisseries awash with decorative stucco bas-relief, brilliant Pompeii reds and flaming ochre yellows, lined with cream-coloured friezes and intricate balconies overhung with fragrant garlands of roses and carved eagles. The town is a riotous succession of Biedermeier-style villas and old-fashioned spa hotels, but such lavish architecture comes as no surprise, especially when one learns that Opatija was the holiday hotspot for royalty from the Austro-Hungarian Empire.

PAGE 86: *The old town of Rab is best viewed from one of the elegant Renaissance buildings that overlook the whole town.*

OPPOSITE: *A bronze statue on the sea-front promenade that links Opatija to Lovran is a romantic reminder of the town's past.*

THIS PAGE: *The shining deep blue splendour of the picturesque Kvarner Gulf easily rivals that of the famed Italian Riviera.*

It all began in the early 19th century when Iginio Scarpa, a rich industrialist from Rijeka, came to Opatija, which was at the time little more than a few houses huddled around the Church of St Jacob. On seeing how the modest village was surrounded by the deep blue sea, and had a winter climate never dropping below 10°C (50 °F), he immediately fell in love with the place. He built the Villa Angiolina, named after his wife, on its shores, with a large garden he filled with exotic plants. Incidentally, the adjacent residence, the 'Ballerina's Villa', was built by Kaiser Franz-Josef for a dancer-friend.

As in St Tropez, the trend was set. During the 1850s, the ban, the Croatian court's representative, frequented Opatija with his wife, followed by other courtiers. At the end of the decade, the crowned heads of Europe were present in full force—the Archduke Ferdinand, Empress Marie-Anne, Kaiser Franz-Josef, the Duke of Savoy, Russian nobles and the Hohenzollerns. Illustrious figures such as the great composers Puccini and Mahler, writer James Joyce and dancer Isadora Duncan also flocked there. Two worlds, fishermen and Imperial Vienna, rubbed shoulders without mingling.

The Belle Époque façade of the seafront Hotel Quarnero was completed in 1910. A century later, its terraces are still lapped by blue waves. It was built for the Austro-Hungarian nobility, and its ballroom still echoes with Strauss' Viennese waltzes.

THIS PAGE : *The lovely landscaped gardens of the Villa Angiolina have retained the original early 20th-century layout and designs over newer garden fashions.*

OPPOSITE (FROM TOP): *A coffee break in the charming town of Lovran is a moment to be savoured; Lovran's houses are huddled together in a town plan that converges dually towards the local church and the sea.*

Lungomare, a 12-km (7-mile) shaded seafront promenade which links Volosko to Lovran via Opatija, was created so that visitors could benefit from the robust, bracing sea air during walks. Strolling along Lungomare was declared healthy by 19th-century respiratory specialists back then, and so clinics, thermal and health establishments (precursors of modern thalassotherapy centres) thrived. As was the fashion in Baden-Baden or Marienbad, 'taking the water in Opatija' became a must, conveniently placed as it was near Vienna. At the time, there was a direct railway from Rijeka to Vienna which transported Austria's aristocracy to the coast in under eight hours.

Today, sauntering at sunset along the Lungomare has become a local habit. In the heat of the day, when not taking cures, people relax in the park in the shade of the pine-trees or lounge in the many Viennese cafés. Laurels, fig-trees, palm-trees, cherry-trees, chestnuts, bamboo, cypresses and fragrant roses all flourish here. The highly advantageous combination of Mediterranean and mainland create a microclimate which is stable and mild all year round.

lovran, the lovely land of laurel

Named for the laurel trees that are abundant everywhere, Lovran is a continual festival of fruity smells, plants and wild species such as cherries, chestnuts, green asparagus, and varieties of mushrooms. A small seaside resort, a port and a medieval town lying in the shadow of Opatija, Lovran too has its own discreet charm and turn-of-the-century villas with verdant gardens lining the seafront, perfectly restored to modern standards, such as the elegant Villa Astra, now a charming small hotel with a pool and spa. The town was once the residence of Roman patricians. Now, visitors enter the walled medieval city

via the postern gate. The main square is surrounded by 17th- and 18th-century baroque houses and a medieval tower. Above the entrance to the Church of St George, the patron saint is shown slaying his eternal dragon.

volosko, fresh fish all around

Volosko is a fishing village huddled behind a port, its stark canvasses of white houses adorned with blind arcades, adapting simple Mediterranean architecture to provide elegant abodes for rich shipowners. Along the jetty, restaurants vie for custom. One such establishment, the Plavi Podrum, with its motto 'honest wine and fresh fish', is considered one of the best restaurants in Croatia. Their menu is a list of the best: red mullet, monkfish, John Dory, sea bass—all fished locally and freshly prepared. Traditional dishes such as rockfish soup and boiled rascasse with seaweed polenta are held in high regard.

the kvarner islands

On Krk, don't miss Kosljun, an islet with a monastery on it, reached by taxi boat from the port of Punat. A short ten-minute crossing separates the bustle of Punat's crowds and souvenir sellers from the peace and tranquillity of this Franciscan monastery, a haven with a collection of sacred art and 20 rooms for those in search of spiritual renewal.

On Krk, squid and cuttlefish abound and the traditional fisherman's fry-up is flavoured with rosemary and bay leaf. Baska surlice (long, thin pasta tubes) are made here, eaten with lamb goulash. The island of Cres is famous for its salt-marsh lamb. In the Gorski Kotar region, frogs' legs and game with mushroom sauce are popular. Wash them down with some white Krizol, made from white Susak grapes, or a cool sparkling wine from Bakar.

cres and losinj, legendary islands

Cres and Losinj are two islands linked by an isthmus—a thin ribbon of rock running for 99 km (62 miles) alongside the mainland, and they are often treated as a single entity. One theory of their origins goes back to Greek mythology, the legend of the Argonauts.

THIS PAGE: Fishing is one of the main activities carried out along the Kvarner coastline.

OPPOSITE: The origin of the island of Cres is linked to the Greek legend of the Golden Fleece.

Back in the 3rd century BCE, Jason and the Argonauts were busy fleeing from the Colchians who wanted to get their hands on the precious Golden Fleece. According to ancient legend, their flight brought them to the Kvarner region. Perfidious Medea, who was in love with Jason, guided her brother, Apsyrtos, to her lover's hideout. But Jason outwitted Apsyrtos and killed him. Medea subsequently cut his body into several pieces and scattered them into the sea, whereupon they were then miraculously transformed into a cluster of islands. Therefore, what the ancient Greeks commonly referred to as the Apsirtides is actually the present-day archipelago of Cres and Losinj.

...relaxing pavement cafés and picturesque beaches with umbrellas.

Although linked by both geography and history, these islands are as different as chalk and cheese. Cres stretches 60 km (40 miles) from tip to tip, twice as long as Losinj. While both islands are covered with biking and hiking trails, Cres is a haven for campers and hikers who prefer to rough it out, while Losinj, on the other hand, is the island of choice for yachters, leisure-seekers and tourists looking around for relaxing pavement cafés and picturesque beaches with umbrellas. More than half of Cres is awkwardly covered with rocks and tough scrub grass, an unfriendly terrain that is interrupted only by the intersecting rock fences and sheep shelters. Losinj, however, is generously blanketed with a thick tree cover, well-groomed white pebble beaches, a wide variety of interesting shops and restaurants, and several large resort hotels.

Prehistoric people have been found to have existed in Osor, where the islands meet. They were followed by the Illyrians, the Greeks and the Romans who called the place Apsoros. History has been built in consecutive layers at Osor—on the same sacred site, pre-Christian pagan tombs and megaliths are found deep beneath Roman temples and fortifications, which were in their turn built over in the 15th century by the Cathedral of Our Lady. Today, Osor is a charming, small, peaceful village whose rose-covered squares host a well-reputed summer music festival where locals and visitors flock in the warm months.

OPPOSITE: With so much sky and sea, it is difficult to tell where the mainland ends and the islands start. Looking out from Cres, the mainland looms on the horizon.

THIS PAGE (FROM TOP): The pebbles carpeting the seabed prevent the cloudy water of sand beaches; at night, the port of Mali Losinj resembles a mini St Tropez, filled with glamorous sailing yachts and motorboats that come in every day to dock at its quay.

kvarner's mainland

Behind Opatija lies Mount Vojak and its cool wooded slopes. The surrounding low foothills are traversed by numerous footpaths leading up through cork-oak and chestnut woods to clearings, belvederes with breathtaking views over the gulf. These walks are especially popular in the summer months.

gorski kotar, nature's open book

The mountainous region of Gorski Kotar lies just by the Slovenian border, with the main road that leads from the capital Zagreb to Rijeka running closely along its southern edge. It is a land of extremes, of old stone-built cathedrals and deep weathered-rock canyons, deep lakes and forests of evergreen fir trees, of dizzying heights and vertiginous plummets. A sanctuary for the wild indigenous animals and plants, it is the kingdom of the brown bear, but also of trout fishing and skiing, with many fashionable ski-resorts in the vicinity, such as Rudnik, Delnice and the Olympic training centre at Bjelolasica, with its peak culminating at 1,534 m (5,033 ft).

the velebit mountain range, a world biosphere reserve

The Velebit massif lies parallel to the Adriatic sea, opposite the islands of Rab and Pag. The coastal side looks like vast sand dunes reflected in the sea, while the other side is forested as far as the eye can see. The contrast is striking. For the most part growing wild, with just the odd rustic hamlet scattered here and there, the Velebit region is purely the domain of nature lovers and solitary shepherds. Stretching 150 km (93 miles) in length, it is also the largest area on the UNESCO World Heritage list.

a land of stone...

Karst is a geological phenomenon that is most prevalent in Croatia. It is a highly porous limestone and dolomitic rock that recurs throughout the Kvarner region. In its natural state it is still

commonly used every day for building low walls (gromace) in the Veli Mrgav and Baska districts. When aerially viewed, landscapes edged with these walls resemble nothing else as much as an abstract modern painting. Karst walls separate, grey on green, dwellings from farmland and pastures, and are a sure sign one is in rural Croatia. When cut, karst is also used for building houses and other structures in the small countryside villages and paving their narrow village lanes. As a highly sought-after and versatile sculptural material, it has been used since olden times, as the many roughly carved statues and columns periodically unearthed in the area will testify.

Full of local character, 'The Devil's Pass' and the 'Green Whirlpool' are regional names of caves and sinkholes found in the Vrela, Gorski Kotar and Lokvarka districts, offering tantalising hints at unexplored mysteries deep within the earth. Pale and light, the Velebit cliffs shimmer like a mirage falling into the sea.

...and water

Water from the mountains traverses kilometres of karst formations on its winding way to the sea where it finally mingles with the salty Mediterranean Sea. The abundant springs are nonetheless capricious. While some islands, such as Rab, have over 300 sources of fresh water, others have all too few, and some, such as the small island of Susak, receive no water at all.

OPPOSITE: The rugged surfaces of the karstic cliffs are perfect for activities such as rock climbing.

THIS PAGE (FROM TOP): The Goranska region is famous for skiing and snowboarding in the winter, with its own Olympic centre, and for fishing and hiking in summer; with a bit of luck, one may be able to spy a brown bear in its habitat—wooded heights of the Gorski Kotar mountain range.

Lake Vransko on the island of Cres is a unique and curious natural phenomenon, a large area of clear, fresh water located right in the middle of a surrounding sea of salt. Seen as a geological near-miracle, it is a perfect reservoir that provides most of the drinking water for the residents on both the islands of Cres and Losinj.

Rijeka, which has its etymological roots in the Croatian word for 'river', lies directly above a complex web of concealed underground waterways and unsuspected streams. Not in the least surprisingly, the town's coat of arms is a double-headed eagle standing on a vessel from which a stream of water flows abundantly, a veritable aquatic cornucopia.

glagolitic script

Glagolithic script is the oldest known alphabet, literally carved in stone, and invented more than a thousand years ago by St Cyril and St Methodius in order to translate the Latin Bible and other texts into the Slavic languages. The verb 'glagolyati' ('to speak' in regional dialect) gives its name to this fascinating constructed ancient alphabet, which is written and well-documented but, with the exception of a few erudite monks of obscure learning, not spoken.

The most important records from the 11th to 15th centuries are all written in glagolitic script—stone inscriptions, numerous and unique to the Kvarner region. There are still plenty of examples of these texts with their rounded script found on slabs of moss-covered stone, especially in and around the village of Vrbnik on the island of Krk, but also on the islands of Cres, Losinj and Rab. The most important example of this alphabet is the Baska Tablets, carved in the 12th century, which originally formed part of the paving stones in the Church of St Lucy in Jurandvor, near Baska (the original of the earlier and better preserved of these two tablets is in the Croatian Academy of Arts and Sciences in Zagreb). For those interested in finding out more about this unique script, there is a permanent exhibition of glagolitic culture in the library in Rijeka.

THIS PAGE: Cres at sunset—the perfect time for cooling off in the Adriatic after the day's heat.

OPPOSITE: A symphony of jewel-like colours—the emerald green of Rab island set off against the surrounding turquoise of the shallows and sapphire sea.

PAGES 100 AND 101: Visitors enjoy a day trip on the island of Krk.

A geological miracle...

Hotel Villa Astra

At the height of its power, the mighty Austro-Hungarian Empire encompassed about 18 different countries and controlled much of Central Europe, from the Alps in the west to the Ukraine in the east. With so much territory under their command, the Empire's ruling elite were privy to the crème de la crème of the continent's select destinations, often establishing their choices as well-recognised holiday spots to the present day. One of their favourite resorts happened to be the small seaport of Lovran on the Opatija Riviera on the beautiful Adriatic coast of Croatia.

For those who have visited the town before, this will come as no surprise. Lovran's superb location offers everything that a world-class holiday destination should, combining a rich and romantic maritime history, well-preserved medieval architecture and great natural beauty with a splendid year-round Mediterranean climate—not to mention a first-class culinary tradition and a highly accessible and convenient geographical position within Europe. Last but not least, the town enjoys the various benefits of having a water supply whose health-giving qualities are famous throughout the whole region—one of the leading factors which led to the town's development by the Austro-Hungarians in the first place.

This unique combination of fortuitous circumstances appealed to Lovranske Vile, a Croatian-based company that specialises in providing holiday villas and hotels that blend natural and cultural heritage with a warm personal environment and high levels of comfort. Founded in 1996, following the political changes that opened the country to tourism, they found properties that, with some investment and careful renovation, could be brought back to their former glory.

THIS PAGE (FROM TOP): The hotel was completed in 1905 in lush Venetian Floral Gothic style; the exterior surface and windows of the villa are richly ornamented and well preserved; bathroom interiors are fully modern and tasteful.

OPPOSITE (FROM LEFT): The Restaurant Villa Astra's Hungarian Room; the Room Josip on the first floor is warmly dressed in various soothing shades of green.

Now, a mere 10 years later, one of the destinations that they offer is the Hotel Villa Astra. Originally completed in 1905 in Venetian Floral Gothic style, this magnificent boutique hotel overlooking the sea offers six double rooms on both a short break and long stay basis. Facilities here include an outdoor pool charmingly set within an artistically landscaped garden, a feature in its own right. A wellness centre offers a full range of relaxing massage therapies and other body treatments for the discerning, including reflexology and traditional massages from India, Guam and Bali.

The Hotel Villa Astra is perhaps most notable for an exceptional gourmet restaurant that specialises in Mediterranean cuisine, and can proudly lay claim to both top international chefs and one of the best wine cellars in the region. Outstanding local in-house specialities include signature dishes that involve freshly harvested cherries, chestnuts, and wild asparagus, as well as freshly caught seafood, all expertly prepared according to tradition and the season.

Tempting as it might be, guests at the Villa Astra would be ill-advised to stay within the confines of the hotel, no matter how luxurious and comfortable they find it. After all, the nearby town and surrounding countryside are a part of what makes this destination so special—which no visit to the area is complete without exploring.

FACTS

ROOMS	6 double rooms
FOOD	Restaurant Villa Astra: Mediterranean
DRINKS	hotel bar
FEATURES	outdoor pool • wellness centre
BUSINESS	meeting room
NEARBY	Lovran
CONTACT	V.C. Emina 11, 51415 Lovran • telephone: +385.51.294 400 • facsimile: +385.51.294 600 • email: villa.astra@lovranske-vile.com • website: www.lovranske-vile.com

PHOTOGRAPHS COURTESY OF LOVRANSKE VILE.

Hotel Arbiana

The small Adriatic island of Rab, just off the northern Croatian coast, has been a favourite destination for Europe's high society for more than a hundred years. Yet, despite its enduring popularity, it retains all of the character and pristine natural beauty that made it such a hotspot in the first place. Add to this the fact that the island has some of the finest weather in all of Europe, that it is blessed with some of the continent's clearest waters and most beautiful beaches, that it has a depth of history and heritage that incorporates the Roman, Byzantine, Venetian and Austro-Hungarian empires, and it's clear that Rab will continue to be popular for many more years to come.

Throughout its long and illustrious role as a host to the rich and famous, there has only ever been one hotel to stay at during any visit to the island: the Hotel Arbiana in the small medieval walled town of Rab. Situated on the foreshore, this hotel can trace its history back to 1924 when it first opened as the Hotel Bristol, quickly earning a reputation for elegance and excellence which continues to this day.

The Hotel Arbiana offers 28 rooms, including four suites and a presidential suite, all of which have been recently refurbished and are decorated to the highest standards of luxury and comfort. Air-conditioning, satellite LCD television sets and wireless Internet access are standard, and private balconies offer spectacular views of the emerald Adriatic Sea in one direction, while other rooms overlook the old town, with its 13th-century cathedral, four imposing bell towers and Romanesque architecture.

The hotel's San Marino restaurant offers gourmet dishes of Adriatic, Mediterranean and international origin—with a strong

THIS PAGE (CLOCKWISE FROM LEFT): The magnificent view of the town; beautiful weather beckons guests; the colour palette is warm and inviting, a theme repeated throughout the hotel décor.
OPPOSITE: Detailed close-ups of the guestrooms reveal a quiet luxury characteristic of the hotel.

emphasis on 'slow food' using the freshest locally sourced organic ingredients. The restaurant also offers a large selection of the finest wines to accommodate each and every taste, and the Bristol Bar and a separate lounge bar provide the perfect settings for a pre-dinner aperitif or a post-dinner drink. For those wishing to plan a business meeting, wedding reception or some other social function, the hotel also boasts a substantial conference room that can comfortably cater for up to 60 people.

However, as enchanting as every aspect of the Arbiana experience is, guests of the hotel are strongly encouraged to allow a little time to take in the sights and sounds of the surrounding town, including its museums, its 2,000 years of historical attractions and its many cultural festivals. Similarly, the surrounding landscape offers plentiful opportunity for hiking, swimming and other sporting activities. It is for all these reasons that this island is known amongst the locals as 'the pearl of the Adriatic'.

PHOTOGRAPHS COURTESY OF HOTEL ARBIANA.

FACTS		
	ROOMS	23 rooms • 4 suites • 1 presidential suite
	FOOD	San Marino: international fine dining
	DRINKS	Bristol Bar • lounge bar
	FEATURES	disabled access • Internet connection
	BUSINESS	conference room
	NEARBY	four bell-towers of Rab • Church of the Holy Weeping Cross • Church of St. Christopher • Prince Palace • art galleries • Vox Disco • San Antonio Club • Beach Club Santos • Komrcan Park • Velebit National Park
	CONTACT	Obala Petra Kresimira 12, 51280 Rab • telephone: +385.51.775 900 • facsimile: +385.51.775 991 • email: sales@arbianahotel.com • website: www.arbianahotel.com

Istravino Wines

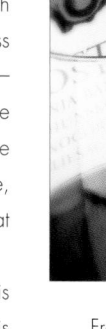

The wines of Burgundy, Bordeaux, South Africa and California are well known across the world and have been for generations—now there is a new player on the scene. The wines of Croatia are beginning to join these esteemed grand-dames on the world stage, and innovative wineries like Istravino are at the forefront of this exciting development.

Headquartered in Rijeka, Istravino is one of the oldest wineries in Croatia. This beautiful country is now more accessible than ever, with an increase of flights coming through every year. The country's coasts are no strangers to winemaking, as vinicultural traditions were strongly established in that region in ancient times. Available throughout the country, Istravino's delicious wines are the epitome of just what Croatia's talented winemakers are capable of. Their diverse range includes high-quality dessert, sparkling and aromatic wines of controlled origin, as well as a wide range of spirits and liqueurs. All these products can also be found around the world, with about 30 per cent of Istravino's production now exported to meet the growing global demand.

Croatian wine has a distinctive style all of its own. Its intriguing varieties are certainly not as ubiquitous or familiar as the Cabernet Sauvignon, Merlot or Sauvignon Blanc, but their relative paucity and distinctly unique flavours make them all the more alluring.

From the Plavac Mali varietal comes Postup, a voluptuously fruity wine coaxed forth from fruit grown on the steeply terraced, sea-facing slopes of Postup. For a stylistic comparison, recent research in wine magazine *Decanter* suggests that Plavac Mali is actually closely related to Zinfandel—mainstay of the Californian wine industry. The sun-drenched climate, sea-reflected light and porous soils combine to make Postup the perfect environment in which to cultivate this luscious wine.

THIS PAGE (CLOCKWISE FROM TOP): *The beautiful south Dalmatian town of Ston where Istravino has one of its most prized vineyards; the luxurious Postup red wine; the notoriously difficult soil of the Ston vineyard produces a precious 30,000 bottles' worth of exceptional fruit each year.*

OPPOSITE: *The terraced slopes of Istravino's vineyards are carefully cultivated to consistently bring out the best in each year's crop.*

Garnet red in colour, this jewel-hued noble wine is made from partially overripe and dried grapes. Its berry-laden bouquet overflows with ripe red fruits, and its palate is full and harmonious—a veritably delicious introduction to Croatian reds.

Plavac Mili is a second, drier red wine from the same Plavac Mali grape. Grown in the breezy, coastal regions of Mili and the rather aptly named Vino, on the Pelješac Peninsula, this wine has a distinctive taste that sets it apart from other wines of the same variety. A deep ruby red, Plavac Mili is a wine with a luxurious bouquet and a firm structure, with layered notes of black fruit on the nose and a generous, full palate.

These wines are an ideal complement to any of the local cheeses and cured meats, and truly embody the flavour of Croatia. Visit any of the Istravino wineries in Istria or Dalmatia to get a feel for authentic Croatian wines and to personally experience their full spectrum of rich flavours in situ.

PHOTOGRAPHS COURTESY OF ISTRAVINO WINES.

FACTS

PRODUCTS Croatian wines • liqueurs • spirits • non-alcoholic beverages
FEATURES nation-wide distribution • specialist wines (aromatised, sparkling, dessert) • coastal vineyards
CONTACT Tome Strižića 8, 51000 Rijeka • telephone: +385.51.406 670 • facsimile: +385.51.406 660 • email: info@istravino-rijeka.hr

dalmatia

Kvarner + Islands

Bosnia + Herzegovina

Pag
Olib
Silba
Permuda
Molat

• **Pag**

Zadar

• **Gračac**
Kučinakosa
1445

• **Obrovac**
Kom
1003
Orlovac
1201
Dinara
1530
Jurišinka
674
• **Knin**

Zadar
• **Preko**
Ugljan
Dugi Otok
Ist
Pašman

• **Benkovac**
V. Promina
1147
Bat
1205
1509

**Biograd
na Moru**
Murter
Vodice
V. Glava
542
Svilaja
1508
Drniš
• **Sinj**
1265

Kornat
Žirje
Šibenik-Knin

Šibenik
510
Kozjak
779
Veliki Kabal
1339
890
Trilj

Trogir
Split
Split-Dalmatia
• **Imotski**

Omiš
Miletnjak
1619

Supetar
Brač
1782
Kimet
1536 1314
Makarska
897

Šolta
Sumartin

Hvarski Kanal
Rilit
863

> Adriana, hvar marina hotel and spa
> Riva, hvar yacht harbor hotel
• **Hvar**
Hvar
• **Sućuraj**
Ploče
Metković

> Palmizana Meneghello
Pakleni Islands
Šćedro

• **Vis**
Korčulanski Kanal
• **Orebić**

Vela Luka
• **Korčula**
Vis
Korčula
Pelješac
Lastovski Kanal
Mljet
Šipan
Lopud
Dubrovnik

Lastovo

**Dubrovnik-
Neretva**

> Hotel Vestibul Palace
> Le Méridien Lav Split

> Hotel Sv Mihovil
> Hotel Šipan
> Hotel Glavovic

> Hilton Imperial Dubrovnik
> Hotel Bellevue
> Hotel Dubrovnik Palace
> Hotel Excelsior
> Pucic Palace
> Villa Dubrovnik
> Dubrovnik House Gallery
> Jewellery Gallery Đardin
> Nautika

**Adriatic
Sea**

N

0 km   20   40   60 km

Legend

☰	Highways
▬	Main roads
—	Other roads
⣿	Proposed road
═	Road under construction
⊕	Airport
⬤	Urban area
◯	Lake
⬤	1500 - 2000 m
⬤	1000 - 1500 m
⬤	500 - 1000 m
⬤	200 - 500 m
⬤	100 - 200 m

the magic of dalmatia

Dalmatia forms a long wedge between the Adriatic and the Dinaric Alps, bordering Bosnia and Herzegovina, 400 km (249 miles) from Zadar in the north to Dubrovnik in the south, with a 25-km (15-mile) strip continuing all the way down to the Montenegro border. All along the coast are ancient cities, open-air museums now classified as World Heritage Sites, ports and fishing villages. Offshore, a myriad of islands, each one as interesting as the others, are scattered out along the full length of the coast.

wandering around zadar

Zadar can be likened to a bottomless treasure box, or a fascinating tapestry woven of art and history. Situated on a narrow peninsula, the walled town is entered through 'Land Gate', a triple-arched gateway above which rides St Chrysogonus, the town's patron saint, and the winged lion of St Mark, emblem of the city of the Doges.

At sunset, its arcaded façade, so typical of late Romanesque architecture, appears at its best, seeming to float, light and golden, beneath skies in swathes of brilliant topaz and crimson. The cathedral is just one out of the many historical monuments found here, which, over the centuries, have occupied the square which was once the Roman forum. Where once there stood temples and pagan gods, there now stands the 13th-century cathedral, alongside the circular mass of the 9th-century Church of St Donat, a blend of Carolingian and Byzantine architectural influences. Set slightly back from the others, the Church of St Mary has a Renaissance façade and a wonderful rococo interior.

The square is a unique space, interspersed with stumps of columns, floor slabs and sculpted sarcophagi, remnants of an ancient temple that still juts out of the ground here and there and which dates back to the origins of Zadar. It is also a favourite meeting place for students as they gather in groups, chatting and making plans for the evening ahead while leaning against walls which once saw Roman legions marching by—a striking tableau of past, present and future. Embroidered shawls and brightly-coloured tablecloths are piled high on stalls set up on the ancient paving stones.

PAGE 108: *Dalmatia's coastline is given over to seaside leisure.*

OPPOSITE: *Each indentation of Hvar island harbours a creek.*

THIS PAGE (FROM TOP): *Small beaches can be found all along the coast; Zadar's main town square is an architectural melting-pot.*

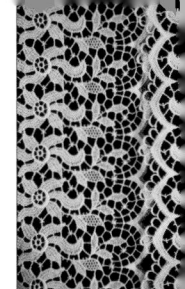

pag, the island of lace

What is the inspiration behind the ethereal beauty of the lace made by the women of Pag? Could it be something in the island's mineral-composition, in the patterns traced by the stone walls demarcating the windswept landscape, in the star-shaped salt crystals which form in the slightest rock indentation? Whatever it is, there appears to be a definite osmotic correlation between the land and the skill of these lacemakers. Ladies at the Austrian court were mad about Pag lace. In Croatia, all well-to-do households had their own live-in lacemaker. A handful of old ladies on Pag still make these precious pieces, but they are the last of a dying trade, their skilful work increasingly replaced by crudely made crochet work using synthetic threads, which is much more quickly produced to meet the fast-paced tourist demand.

šibenik and the discreet charm of the bourgeoisie

The French writer and journalist Elemir Bourges, in *Les oiseaux s'envolent et les fleurs tombent*, sees in Šibenik an air of antiquity: 'a maze of narrow lanes, stairways, alleys between houses with barred windows... and heavy doors clad in metal fittings with engraved knockers.' Unlike much of Croatia, Šibenik was not founded until the 7th century by Croats. The town was inevitably tossed around between the country's many successive invaders: Ottomans, Venetians, Hungarians, French and Austrians. Despite all this, and the heavy bombing during the Second World War, the old part of Šibenik has survived. As has the pleasure of wandering along the lanes and alleys which fan out from each other, of stumbling across the time-worn façade of an elegant mansion or the secret garden of a priory, of idling away time in a small café alongside a chapel. In the glimmer of the street lamps, delicate medieval stone carvings are vividly brought to life—a noble coat of arms above a doorway, a drinking trough for dogs beside a channel, a weaver's measure still marking the wall on a street corner.

THIS PAGE: Women from Pag and its surrounds flock to Zadar to sell their hand-crocheted wares.

OPPOSITE (FROM TOP): Lace is hand-made by the few artisans still in possession of this dying skill; a panoramic view of Šibenik, with typically Croatian urban architecture—houses of pale stone and red-tiled roofs.

"a maze of narrow lanes, stairways, alleys between houses with barred windows..."

THIS PAGE: *Šibenik is deservedly proud of its town cathedral, a UNESCO World Heritage Site.*

OPPOSITE (FROM TOP): *A Dalmatian gravely examines the sculpted figures of the cathedral apse; Primosten's little harbour is characteristic of the island— charming in its simplicity.*

In Šibenik, during the transition between the Gothic and the Renaissance periods, notably in the 15th century, art was very much in the service of the church. The most striking example of the outstanding profession of faith at that period is the St James' Cathedral, now a World Heritage Site. It is largely the work of two Croat sculptor-architects, the talented Juraj Dalmatinac (George the Dalmate, also known as Giorgio Orsini) and his disciple Nikola Firentinac (Nicholas the Florentine). Dalmatinac was largely responsible for bringing the Renaissance to the Adriatic. The technique used for

constructing the dome, without any mortar between the stones, remains a miracle of balance even today. Dalmatinac drew on the local inhabitants and bourgeoisie of his time for inspiration to create this stylistic exercise. All around the outside of the apse are the lively sculptures of 72 characters, their faces frozen in stone, with strikingly realistic features staring down intensely. Among the most remarkable are those of the husband, wife and mistress, illustrating the eternal themes of seduction and deception.

one stop, two stops...

A short boat row, or more likely a quick ride on the water-bus which runs from Bordarica, near Šibenik, brings one to the island of Krapanj, the smallest island on the Adriatic, famous for sponge-fishing. Flat as a pancake, this peaceful island has a few truly beautiful beaches and well-known diving spots. It also has a Franciscan monastery with an interesting and extensive collection of sacred art. The best sea sponges are said to be available from the presbytery.

Further on lies the former island of Primosten (island no longer now that it is linked to the mainland by a bridge and a causeway), its village huddled behind walls and its quay providing shelter from the heavy waves, a perfect stopover en route to the Kornati island archipelago and those islands further south. A sort of miniature St Tropez, as yet unknown, and all the better for it.

the adriatic's beauty spots

In an almost fantastical setting, amid waters of unbelievable transparency, the Kornati island archipelago resembles from afar a rope of baroque pearls strung out along the sea. Now a National Park, the islands are exceptionally beautiful and unusually dense, with 147 islands and islets packed in within a distance of less than 300 km (186 miles). During a visit to the archipelago, the writer George Bernard Shaw once wrote 'that on the last day of the Creation, God desired to crown his work, and thus created the Kornati Islands out of tears, stars and breath', a lasting testament to the islands' beauty.

When sailing from island to island—the easiest way to travel around the Kornati group of islands—it feels as if one exists on another planet. Out at sea, a karstic cliff rises up, pleated like a Fortuny dress; in what appears to be the reflection of some cosmic feature, a cluster of creamy islets barely rise above the water's surface. Elsewhere, a piece of rock, streaked in ochre, crumbles onto a beach; occasionally, voluptuous hillocks of celadon green, like moonstone set in gems, rise from the surface, softening the horizon. One sails or glides, depending on the wind, from one isle to the other, mooring in a creek to swim or

coming ashore to picnic. Most of the islands are wild and deserted; some are privately owned; others are sparsely dotted here and there with a few dwellings which share the land and the odd blade of grass with the occasional sheep or two.

Chief among the Kornati is Kornat island, with a hamlet, a chapel and a look-out tower, though it is still fairly monastic when compared to Murter, the only island with hotels, restaurants and some modest fishermen's huts. These huts have a charm of their own, and are so inviting that they are much sought-after, being rented out for princely sums to a new generation of tourists in quest of the Robinson Crusoe experience.

an island, a lighthouse

All the lighthouses along Croatia's Adriatic coast were built by the Austro-Hungarians during the 19th century. Many are no longer operational, and out of the 40 or so originally built, about a dozen have been converted into fully self-sufficient gîtes, providing adventurous holiday-makers with a number of unusual accommodations and the chance to get away from it all in the company of cormorants and porpoises.

OPPOSITE: The Kornati group of islands lies scattered like stars in an earthbound galaxy across the Adriatic; nature at her very best.

THIS PAGE: A solitary lighthouse perched on a rock occasionally comes into view, the birds and passing boats its only company.

trogir, a ship at anchor

Known as Tragyrion (island of goats) in the time of the Greeks, it became Tragurium under the Romans, finally ending up as Trogir with the Croats. This exquisite medieval city is certainly one of the highlights of the Dalmatian coast. Built on an island, but linked to the mainland by two bridges, it resembles a ship at anchor. The smell of spindrift fills the air, which in turn permeates the light Brač stone all around.

'This town is dear to me because it resembles a ship... Between the ramparts and the sea is nothing but a wide, white quay, like a circle of light,' said writer Albert t'Serstevens in *L'Itinéraire de Yougoslavie*. A town also dear to many famous artists,

ABOVE: Not surprisingly, the town of Trogir, an absolute jewel, is a UNESCO World Heritage Site. Home to local artists and craftsmen since the advent of the Middle Ages, it still has an active artistic community.

writers, sculptors, cabinet-makers and stonecarvers who have chosen to set up abode here, establishing various artisan workshops in the town's elegantly restored houses. Trogir was also listed as a World Heritage Site by UNESCO in 1997.

Such artistic proliferation is not recent here. The colourful Gothic polyptychs of the 15th-century artist, Blaz Jurjev, a native of Trogir, were representative of the blossoming artistic movement known as the School of Dalmatia. There was an artistic exchange between Croatia and Italy, and most enlightened Croatian artists trained in Lombardy or Tuscany, where they were inevitably caught up in the newly emerging Renaissance movement. Back on native soil, they reinterpreted Renaissance art in their own way,

creating a new Croat art form. Among the most famous of these artists are Trogir-born sculptor Ivan Duknovic, and fellow sculptors and countrymen Andrija Alesi and Nikola Firentinac (Nicholas the Florentine, pupil of Dalmatinac), living in Trogir in the second half of the 15th century, whose chapel for the town's first bishop, St Ivan of Trogir (or Blessed Orsini), is a masterpiece of Dalmatian Renaissance art. The chapel forms part of the Cathedral of St Lawrence, itself built in 13th century on the town's main square. The Dalmatian sculptor Master Radovan brought Romanesque art to perfection here: his sculpted doorway, flanked by two powerful lions (the symbol of Venice) supporting statues of Adam and Eve is, quite simply put, a marvel.

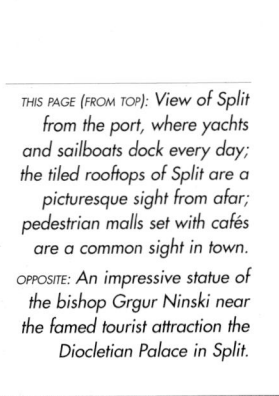

THIS PAGE (FROM TOP): View of Split from the port, where yachts and sailboats dock every day; the tiled rooftops of Split are a picturesque sight from afar; pedestrian malls set with cafés are a common sight in town.

OPPOSITE: An impressive statue of the bishop Grgur Ninski near the famed tourist attraction the Diocletian Palace in Split.

split, a town within a palace

The palace was that of the formidable Roman emperor Aurelius Valerius Diocletianus, otherwise known as Diocletian, which he had built near his hometown of Salona, in the port of Spalatum, later to become Split. It took a grand total of 10 years to finally complete the vast fortified complex—4 hectares (10 acres) in size—built in his image. Waves lapped right up to the foot of the 25-m (82-ft) high ramparts, impressively lined end to end with anchored vessels, where visitors entered the palace through the Bronze Gate into the podrum (the underground chambers).

Reconstitution of the palace's plans, undertaken by the English architect Robert Adam in 1764, brought to light its rigorous layout. The old streets known as Decumanus and Cardo crossed at right angles, separating the buildings into their distinct functions. Diocletian spent the last nine years of

his life there, living in grand and decadent style, full of imperial pomp and ceremony, while carrying out the persecution of early Christians. Dominique Fernandez, in his *Dictionnaire amoureux de l'Italie* observed that 'Diocletian's palace provides one of the most striking examples of Roman splendour…nowhere other than in Piranesi's visions is such grandiose construction matched'.

Not much remains of all that grandeur and decadence today. Almost as reduced as Shelley's Ozymandias, there is only the sacred central square, the peristyle, with columns on three sides, and the vestibule which led to the Emperor's quarters, still watched over by a black granite sphinx, as well as sections of the basement walls of the slaves' quarters, made of brick and pale Brač stone.

Where once lay Diocletian's remains, there now lie those of St Domnius, the first bishop-martyr of Salona, persecuted by order of the Roman emperor. The mausoleum was subsequently transformed into a Christian church in the 7th century, its crypt, a former prison for Christians, dedicated to St Lucy. As for the Temple of Jupiter, it was converted into a baptistry in the 9th century and placed under the protection of St John the Baptist. And all the rest? It's still there, masked by the maze of narrow lanes, on the polished flagstones, in the muddled house façades, in windows opened up in the rampart walls or squashed between columns. Split and its people have built their homes out of the various fragments of the Roman empire.

In 615, fleeing Slav and Avar barbarians, the inhabitants of Salona took refuge within the walls of the palace, by then already abandoned. They took over the imperial apartments, barracks and outbuildings as living quarters, the deserted workshops to work in and installed crosses on those buildings dedicated to imperial cults.

This was the salvation of a palace which soon became the heart of Split, a busy and prosperous trading centre. The town rapidly outgrew its walls and doubled in size. Down through the ages, Gothic-Renaissance palaces grew up in between and fused with existing dwellings. Crowds of visitors thronged into the agora. Various galleries and souvenir shops occupy the vaulted Roman chambers and a new hotel, with very contemporary décor, has opened on the palace steps. Propped up against the outer walls are cafés and their terraces with bright awnings. People stroll up and down the seafront, and its palm-tree lined quay, in true Mediterranean fashion.

brač stone

The pale stone from the island of Brač turns a warm honey colour in the sun, and Pliny the Elder considered it so beautiful that he wrote a tribute to it. Its exceptionally pure grain has the ability to harden on contact with air over time, an exceedingly valuable stone therefore that the Romans extracted in vast quantities from the island's quarries for architectural purposes. It was used to build Split and Trogir, among others, as well as palaces and Gothic cathedrals, and, together with the traditional vermillion-tiled roofs, it gave a light architectural unity to these cities. In its raw state, it readily succumbs to stonecutter's and sculptor's tools in the process of becoming delicate works of art.

The Adriatic's only stonecutting school is found in the village of Pucisca on Brač. Its reserves are seemingly endless, as is its prestige, having been used to build the White House in Washington, the National Parliament Building in Vienna, the Governor's Palace in Trieste and the Parliament Palace in Budapest.

dubrovnik, unique and aristocratic

'Dubrovnik... (the ancient and aristocratic Ragusa) ...owed nominal allegiance to the Emperor at Byzantium until the Fourth Crusade, and after that to Venice... (then the Turks), ...and at the end of the 18th century passed into the hands of the Austrians, but... it remained, aristocratic, and cultured, immeasurably aloof from its savage

THIS PAGE (FROM TOP): Dubrovnik's homage to Orlando, symbol of the city's freedom, and hero of the 11th-century French epic poem Chanson de Roland; the pale stone from the island of Brač is famous for its high quality in ancient and modern works of architecture all over.
OPPOSITE: The magnificent Duke's Palace, situated in Dubrovnik.

'...it remained, aristocratic, and cultured, immeasurably aloof from its savage neighbours.'

neighbours.' The celebrated English man of letters Evelyn Waugh's fine description of Dubrovnik in *Lines: a Mediterranean Journey* very nearly sums up everything that is to be said on what is generally owned to be one of Europe's most beautiful cities.

Literature on Dubrovnik abounds, such has it fascinated writers and aesthetes—and continues to do so. Its history dates back to when it was called Ragusa, a 7th-century fishing village perched on a large rock. Facing the Adriatic Sea, with a mountainous barricade behind, this stronghold was later to become a model of its kind. A small autonomous republic was governed by a priest along with representatives of the local nobility, the church and the merchant classes—a sharing of power wholly new at the time. Skilful negotiations, diplomacy and shrewd tributes allowed Dubrovnik to retain privileged status with the Venetian Republic and Ottoman Empire for over a millennium.

'Sail and trade before all else' was the motto of Ragusa's shipowners in the 15th century. A century later, a fleet of over 200 ships sailed the seas towards Cathay in Asia and Africa. From Occident to Orient, Ragusa bought wood, spices and silks in

OPPOSITE: *Fish—a local favourite.*

BELOW: *Viewed from above, part of Dubrovnik's city walls and the town's main monuments, with the white facade of St John's Fort, which now houses a Maritime Museum, on one side, and the Minceta Tower on the other.*

exchange for salt. Known as "the Athens of the Slav world", and home to high Croat literature and illustrious figures such as the writer Marin Drzic and poet Ivan Gundulic, Ragusa was extremely well placed to pit her culture and wealth against that of her closest rival, Venice. It was indeed the Golden Age of Dubrovnik.

In 1667, an earthquake destroyed the city, followed by the plague and decline. In 1808, Napoleon put an end to the Republic of Ragusa, annexing it as part of the Kingdom of Illyria, placing General Marmont, the Duke of Ragusa, in charge as governor, and bringing the nobility to their knees. The decline continued under the

Austrians, followed by the Communist era and the black years of 1991 to 1995, when Dubrovnik was the theatre for the most tragic and painful events.

Standing on the walkway which surrounds the walled city of Dubrovnik, the writer Jules Romains once professed to hold a deeply rooted admiration of 'the town's multi-coloured rooftops spread out below him, like a sea of shimmering waves.' The acclaimed French writer and scholar Albert t'Serstevens, whose overriding passion for Ragusa was spiritual, sentimental and sensual, observed that there were 'three monasteries, as far away from

one another as possible, undoubtedly due to the old rivalry between their orders. The Franciscan one is at Pile Gate, the Dominican one at the other end of town, beyond Ploce Gate. The Jesuits camped somewhere up on the southern heights.'

The painful evidence of Dubrovnik's appalling war wounds have all but disappeared, thanks to the rapid and extensive restoration work under the aegis of UNESCO, who made the city a World Heritage Site. The tiles given by the French towns of Toulouse and Agen have restored a deep blush to the gutted roofs. Tourists once again flock to the main square and cool themselves with water from the Fountain of Onofrio. Over the stone bridge and the drawbridge they proceed, and through Pile Gate, under the watchful eye of St Blaise, the city's patron saint. Trying not to slip on the white, footworn flagstones, they descend on Placa, the main street, getting

THIS PAGE (FROM TOP): Cool, narrow lanes provide welcome respite from the heat in the daytime; the church bell tower with its elaborate stonework presides tall and proud over Hvar Town like an overseeing lighthouse.

OPPOSITE: Behind many of the crenellated walls in Hvar Town lie elegant palaces and homes.

a feel for the size of the city and admiring the varied mix of architectural styles, from Romanesque to Baroque, while soaking up the unique atmosphere. The city's main artery traverses it from east to west, ending up at Sponza Palace and Ploce Gate—a 300-m (984-ft) axis onto which all the steep, narrow streets converge like streams flowing into a river. Placa was formerly a marshy channel which divided the city into two distinct sections—the nobility to the south, the populace to the north.

Dubrovnik today is a strange blend of the secular and religious. One is hit by the solemnity of the buildings, cloisters, churches, convents and palaces in the foreground, while charmed by the effervescence of the almost Neapolitan activity in the narrow backstreets. It is like watching a theatrical performance from the wings as well as from the stalls. Maybe that is the secret of Dubrovnik's charm, appealing to one's emotions and sentiments at every turn. In the shade of narrow stepped lanes one comes upon inns and restaurants serving delicious local food, in particular the well-known eatery of Trabakula, housed in the former home of one of the town's illustrious figures.

The Elafiti islands, northwest of the city, were annexed by the Republic of Dubrovnik and became a favourite holiday spot for the Ragusan bourgeoisie in the 15th century, whose patrician homes have survived to this very day. The best-known islands out of these are Kolocep, Šipan and Lopud; the latter, a 50-minute boat ride away, still has a number of interesting churches and a bustling little village, a number of fascinating walks and several beautiful, isolated beaches perfect for undisturbed bathing.

hvar, the star

Hvar is a natural stopping-off point for every yacht sailing out of Portofino, just as it was for ships in the old days of the Venetian Republic. Following in the illustrious wake of Princess Caroline of Monaco, Emmanuelle Béart and Steven Spielberg, the jet-set have enthusiastically adopted Hvar for their own. The town's main square, almost as vast and as magical as San Marco's in Venice, is almost like a huge dance floor which everyone glides around, exchanging greetings, sooner or later finding one other. The

...the jet-set have enthusiastically adopted Hvar.

cafés are full to overflowing, their terraces edging ever further out onto the square's paving, made of light Brač stone, but with the exquisite sheen of white marble. Hvar hasn't quite got used to being a star again, for, like Majorca, the place was all the rage in the early days of seaside resorts and bathing.

Both rustic and worldly, bucolic and chic, Hvar is an island of fields. Inland, it is as rugged as ever—strong-smelling dense maquis, rocky mule tracks, abrupt cliffs dropping down to the sea. Elsewhere, there are entire fields where fragrant lavender bushes grow, hillsides overrun with wild herbs, slopes covered with carpets of green vines, and clear creeks. Not surprisingly, many a famous writer has been bowled over by Hvar.

Back in Hvar Town, the port and its marina offer plenty of diversion for leisure-seekers: not only is there an abundance of restaurants, trattorias and konobas, but spiritual replenishment can also be found in the form of a theatre, purportedly Europe's first for the people and aristocracy alike, housed on the first level of the Arsenal building. An unspoken war divided the island's minor bourgeoisie from the Venetian aristocracy. While the high nobles were entertained with chamber music, the islanders had to content themselves with listening from the church forecourt. To calm this brewing indignation, a small theatre was constructed, one in which everyone was admitted, except for women, who had to wait until the late 19th century before being allowed even to attend such entertainment alongside the men.

A slightly different form of spiritual replenishment is found in the Cathedral of St Stjepan housing one of Croatia's oldest icons; the Benedictine monastery where lace is still made from

dried agave leaves; and the garden of the old Franciscan monastery with its 200-year-old cypress tree and painting of the Last Supper, in the refectory, undoubtedly influenced by Leonardo da Vinci's world-famous masterpiece.

Dalmatia's first ever 1900s hotel-palace is still standing, behind a Renaissance façade (a remnant from the earlier 16th-century ducal palace), its bay windows overlooking the sea. Alongside boat-cabins, family-run guesthouses and the old-fashioned charm of a grand hotel with spa, an innovative project is underway to create about a dozen or so establishments which will offer a wider choice of accommodations to cope with the island's changing needs. The first of these boutique hotels, the Riva, with 53 rooms, has just opened in a beautifully restored house on the quayside. Behind its elegant façade of white stone and red roofs, the décor is pleasingly contemporary. Hvar already has nearly everything necessary to satisfy; it will soon have everything necessary to please all as well. It is undoubtedly the most fashionable island in the Adriatic and the most prosperous in Croatia.

The misnamed Pakleni Islands—which mean 'infernal islands'—opposite Hvar, are, in fact, the perfect getaway destination when Hvar itself becomes too crowded. Palmizana is particularly popular, with its myriad of winding footpaths that wend their way through cool pine forests, leading down to pebble beaches and to an unexpected find—a charming hotel and art gallery.

OPPOSITE: *Hvar the star, in the shade of its many laurel trees.*
THIS PAGE (FROM TOP): *Hvar's main square, the Adriatic's largest after San Marco's in Venice, with a white marble fountain and the Cathedral of St Stjepan; inland Hvar is fragrant with lavender, a major economic resource for the island.*

...isolation and enforced self-sufficiency have left the island untouched.

issa the beautiful

Vis is the furthest and most westerly of the Dalmatian islands. The ferry runs between the islands of Solta and Brač, around Hvar and on, before docking two and a half hours later at Luka, the port for Vis Town. Vis itself was a military base from 1945 on, and has only been open to visitors since 1991. This deep isolation and enforced self-sufficiency have left the island very nearly untouched. Or as Paul Morand succinctly puts it: 'The landscape in Vis and Lastovo is as pure as at the dawn of time.'

Vis, however, was not always isolated. In ancient times it was a bustling place, known as Issa to the Greeks, who made it their first trading post in the Adriatic. If the numerous amphorae lining the seabed are anything to go by, the Romans, too, carried out a roaring wine trade there. There are still traces of a Roman road and the ruins of a thermae, now overgrown with wild vegetation. The Croats were not interested in the island and gave it over to a monastic order. The English, however, used it for bypassing Napoleon's naval blockade. During the years of the Second World War, Tito established his headquarters there, on Hum hill, and it then subsequently became a base for the Yugoslav navy. As for the native Isseans, many of them migrated on to better life opportunities in the United States during the 19th century.

The composite town of Vis is made up of two villages, Luka and Kuta, separated by a bay 3 km (2 miles) long, with local islanders' dwellings cheek by jowl with the wealthier abodes. Over on the west coast, in Komiza, there are as many cafés and sobe (rooms to let) as fishing boats, and further around the

OPPOSITE: Vis, the most distant out of all the Dalmatian islands, is entered via its bay just beyond the Benedictine monastery, with the port of Luka at its far end.

THIS PAGE (FROM TOP): The quaint little fishing port of Kuta in Vis; diving off a rock into the warm water thrills both old and young.

coast, miniscule ports, clear creeks and cliffs with nothing but the sea below. Inland is just as magical—hillsides criss-crossed with drystone-walled fields, terraced with vines, olive groves and fruit trees. Small roads peter out in the middle of nowhere or lead to abandoned villages or farms. Wine, however, is still produced on Vis. At harvest time, amidst much festivity, houses transform into winepresses and storerooms. An ethereal smell of grape must pervades the villages and barrels are lined up along the quays.

During the summer, their place is taken by an endless flow of yachts and pleasure boats docking for the night. As the port of Kuta glows fiery red in the sunset, white sails invade the bay and the small restaurants come to life. As one dines under trellised vines by the waterfront, sipping locally produced cool white Vugava, accompanied by a squid ink risotto, one gets the impression of being in one of the last Adriatic hideaways.

korčula the venetian

Although Korčula's origins date back to the Trojan wars, it was the Venetians, who occupied the island as early as the 10th century, who made the most lasting impressions on the place. Covered in acres of green oak, and being rich in limestone, the island soon found its vocation as quarry and shipyard for the city of the Doges. Lumber and quarried stone circulated alongside ideas, and Korčula soon become a cultivated and prosperous city, the most Venetian of the Dalmatian islands.

The street plan of Korčula Town resembles an X-ray of a sea bream with narrow lanes converging towards its backbone. The solidly built houses turn their backs on the bora, the north wind. The central square is dominated by the St Mark's Cathedral, its entrance flanked by two lions. Inside, the wooden ceiling of the nave resembles the upturned great hull of a boat. Several of the altarpiece paintings are attributed to Tintoretto or his workshop.

Like Venice, Korčula also claims to be the birthplace of Marco Polo. His family home lies a few steps from the cathedral and is open to visitors. Coincidentally, Marco Polo was captured by the Genoese during a naval battle in 1298 and was locked up in Korčula where he dreamt up his incredible travel book, *The Book of Wonders*.

The Moreska Sword Dance dates back to the late Middle Ages and mimes the battle between Christian Spaniards and Muslim Moors. In a choreographed dance set to music, the white knight crosses swords with the black knight to win the love of Bula, the ravishing Moor. The Moreska is often performed in the square on summer evenings.

OPPOSITE (FROM TOP): Lion motifs are a familiar sight on Korčula, a reminder of old Venetian rule; before it was a marina, Korčula was a famed shipyard known throughout the Mediterranean.

THIS PAGE: Picturesque Korčula lies just off the Pelješac peninsula.

PAGES 136 AND 137: Korčula seems quietly sleepy, but pulls in vast numbers of tourists each year.

Hotel Vestibul Palace

Split's first boutique hotel, Vestibul Palace has already become a prestigious 'Fodor's Choice' destination, hailed by *Lonely Planet Croatia* as 'Split's most exclusive, in-demand address'. In a youthful and vibrant city impressively brimming with shops, bistros and cafés, this is kudos indeed.

An über-chic, upmarket destination, this hotel was created by the architectural fusion of three ancient palaces, Romanic, Gothic and Renaissance. The result is a unique and daring juxtaposition of rough-hewn exposed stonework and sleek modernity. This unlikely but successful pairing is the basis for Split's most unusual and intimate escape.

With a mere five rooms and two suites, this retro-minimalist rarity is located within the old palace walls, accessed through the 1,700-year-old Roman vestibule itself. With these ancient walls incorporated into the structure of the two suites, the feeling of history permeates the entire building. After long years of meticulous and painstaking restoration, the imaginative Hotel Vestibul Palace has completely rejuvenated this richly historic and culturally important piece of local heritage in the town of Split.

Equipped with plasma screen TVs and Internet connections, the hotel's interior layers modernity over antiquity in deft strokes. Lines are angular with clean smooth edges, with not a single item in each space out of place

to jar the senses of the most acute aesthete. The colour palette is informed by rich and harmonious tones of brown, black and beige. Leather headboards and smooth, hardwood floors are complemented by handmade furniture made by local artisans. Striking against the simplicity of the bare

THIS PAGE (CLOCKWISE FROM ABOVE): *The hotel's private open courtyard; an aerial view of the compound; the Restaurant Vestibul is light and airy, welcoming guests.*

OPPOSITE (FROM LEFT): *The minimalist elegant lounge area is furnished sleekly, ideal for quiet nights in; natural colour tones softly blend into the hotel's structure, built out of centuries-old stonework.*

stone walls and hardwood floors, these elements add up to one of the most stylish experiences to be found in the entire city.

Detailed finishing touches are to be found in the reversible fine silk covers on the beds, turned down in the evenings by discreet and professional staff who leave chocolates and the coming weather report on the pillows. Even the bathtubs are sleekly angular, designed with aesthetic flair.

In the lobby, Le Corbusier armchairs and other inspired designer touches are shown to their best advantage by the natural light pouring through the glass roof. An exposed Roman wall divides the black Japanese porcelain-potted palms of the ground-floor café from the Restaurant Vestibul, where muted conversations are carried out amongst the exposed stones, each of which has its own story to tell.

Out in the World Heritage-protected city, the gleaming whitewashed stones of the ancient buildings reflect the warm intermittent glow of the street lamps in the balmy summer evenings. A few steps away is hidden one of the smallest and oldest cathedrals in the world. For a unique experience in the heart of one of the most fascinating urban landscapes in the world, the Hotel Vestibul Palace is the best place to start.

FACTS		
	ROOMS	5 rooms • 2 suites
	FOOD	Restaurant Vestibul: international
	DRINK	Café Vestibul
	FEATURES	plasma TV screens • Internet connection • marble bathrooms
	NEARBY	St. Duje Cathedral • Emperor Diocletian's mausoleum • Jupiter's temple • City Museum • Croatian National Theatre • City Youth Theatre • local markets
	CONTACT	Iza Vestibula 4, 21000 Split • telephone: +385.21.329 329 • facsimile: +385.21.329 333 • email: info@vestibulpalace.com • website: www.vestibulpalace.com

PHOTOGRAPHS COURTESY OF HOTEL VESTIBUL PALACE.

Le Méridien Lav Split

8 km (5 miles) away from the city centre, the hotel's distinctive panoramic sea views are literally unsurpassed for miles around.

With eight separate restaurants offering cuisine drawing inspiration from around the world, eight further bars and cafés and extensive shopping, sporting, business and leisure facilities, Le Méridien Lav Split's four interlinked buildings are an ideal way to escape, away from it all in holiday bliss.

An adrenaline rush is never far away; water sports, scuba diving, tennis, and rock climbing are simply a few of the hotel's extensive menu of activities on offer.

Shopaholic guests will most certainly appreciate the exclusive boutiques at the marina's shopping centre. The dedicated Penguin Children's Club will happily occupy little minds and hands, allowing full-scale credit card splurges to continue unhindered. Outside on the impressive and graceful

Split is the perfect gateway to Croatia and the yachting capital of the Adriatic. This 1,700-year-old UNESCO World Heritage city fuses a turbulent past with prospects of a bright future to create a positively buzzing present. The ideal spot from which to launch an exploration of the bustling city and its lovely surroundings, Le Mériden Lav Split is the city's premier luxury resort hotel. Split's only fully integrated hotel complex, Le Méridien Lav Split is surrounded by beautiful landscaped gardens created by the award-winning designer Jim Nicolay. Located on a private stretch of white, sandy beach a mere

THIS PAGE (FROM TOP): A dazzling view of Le Méridien Lav Split; a luxuriously appointed room.

OPPOSITE: Le Méridien's extensive fitness complex includes a gym, indoor pool and spa, indicating yet again Le Méridien's strong commitment to guests' well-being.

...the ideal spot from which to launch an exploration of the bustling city...

Marina Promenade, no fewer than 60 glistening super yachts bob alongside the shops, restaurants and bars of the harbour. Serious spenders—or curious dabblers—will be tempted to visit the Grand Casino Lav, the only one of its kind in Croatia. Prepare to be magnetised by the busy poker and roulette tables or enter the exclusive Salon Privé. Whether player or spectator, all of the Casino visitors are welcome to enjoy a drink in the lively Sports Bar or the hotel's adjoining InMotion nightclub, popular with the city's fashionable and glamorous.

If inner calm and serenity is a priority, the Diocletian Spa and Wellness Centre offers a wide range of treatments and

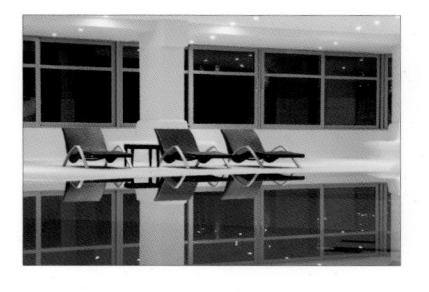

facilities, including a Tepidarium, several pools, saunas, steam baths, stimulating cold plunge pools and adventure showers. For the meditative, customised packages await in the relaxation zone. Herbal walks, aqua safaris and yoga are popular selections. To encourage this feeling of space and inner calm, the hotel boasts the largest guestrooms on the Dalmatian coast. The warm, inviting guestrooms and public areas have been created by famed Italian designer Lorenzo Bellini specifically for Le Méridien Lav and are exquisitely equipped to the latest and highest global standards in order to ensure a luxurious and comfortable stay.

The impressive list of technological gadgetry that welcomes each guest includes flat-screen and plasma multi-channel TVs, high-speed Internet access and personalised climate control in each room. In many of the suites, private jacuzzis and well-placed balconies with amazing views of the nearby islands are standard features. The library has been designed for those seeking a spot of

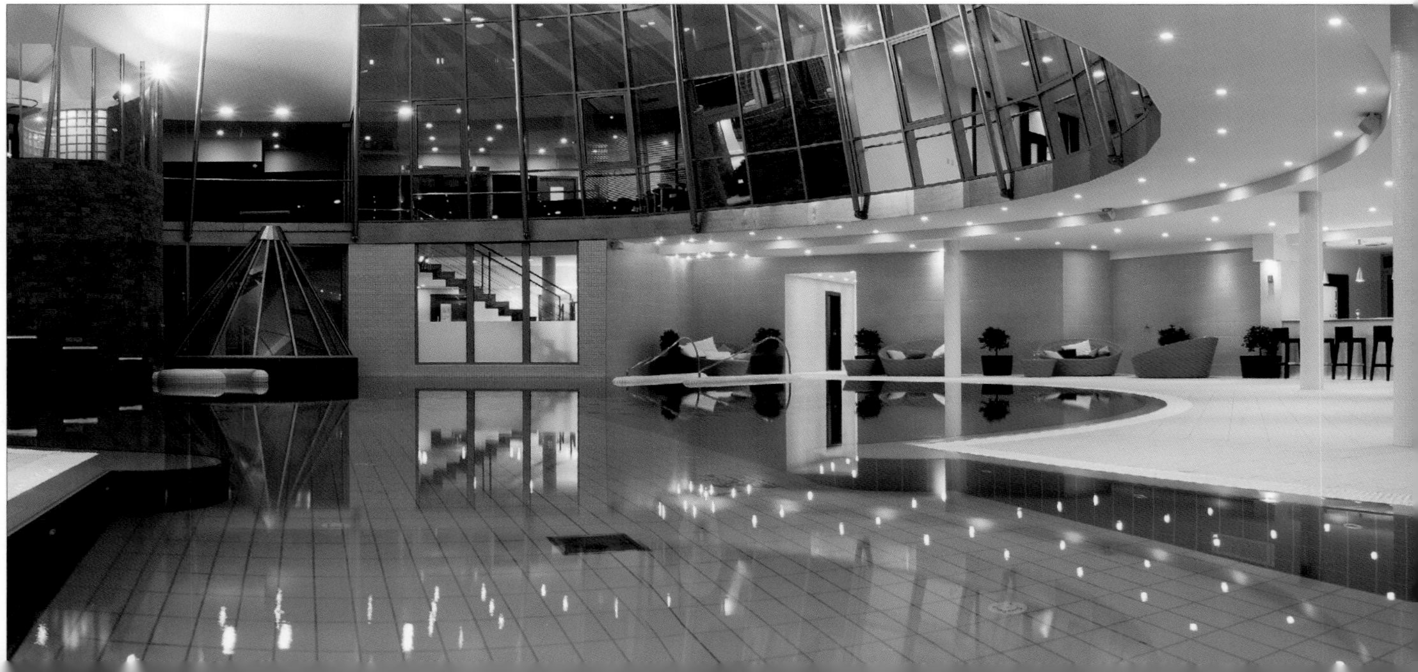

THIS PAGE (CLOCKWISE FROM ABOVE): The Spalatum Galleria serves up exquisite cuisine to guests daily; The hotel's chic Champagne Bar; relax in the steaming whirlpool.

OPPOSITE (FROM LEFT): The hotel spa's Aroma Grotto where guests can seek—and find—rejuvenation; low lights set the atmosphere in the Tepidarium's relaxing zone.

self-enrichment amongst all this luxury and indulgence. Select from a range of classic and contemporary books before sinking into a comfortable chair, or simply relax in a quiet corner of this tranquil sanctum. Also available on their day of publication are international newspapers and magazines. After all, 'out of town' does not have to mean 'out of touch'.

Borrow a book on Croatian art, then retire to the comfort of the Art Café to enjoy it over a steaming cup of coffee. A venue decorated with works of sought-after regional contemporary artists, it also boasts the largest selection of teas and coffees in the country, and an array of irresistible Dalmatian dainties such as mini cakes and sweet pastries.

Le Méridien is renowned for its investment in people, exemplified by the immaculate comportment of its staff. As in the

Art Café, local cultural achievements and causes are championed, the concierge keen to recommend to guests all the particularly interesting events and highlights of the local arts calendar, from musical performances to fashion shows and art gallery exhibitions.

The delightful atmosphere, activities and accommodations considered, now to the most memorable part of Le Méridien Lav— the cuisine. Gastronomic innovation, fine wines, and impeccable service: these are the elements around which the hotel's restaurants revolve. Fine dining venues include the Spalatum Galleria restaurant, open daily for breakfast, lunch and dinner. Its open plan kitchens theatrically showcase the artistic culinary manoeuvres of the restaurant chef to appreciative diners; the international menu is almost guaranteed to delight all palates.

The Spalatum Brasserie allows its à la carte menu to speak for itself. Select a fine Croatian wine from the prodigiously stocked cellar before adjourning to the open-air terrace to enjoy its nuanced bouquet. New research suggests that California's Zinfandel wine grape is actually Croatian in origin, closely related to the celebrated indigenous varieties Plavac Mali and Crljenak.

Those who relish the nightlife will be pleased to discover that Le Méridien Lav has a bar for every occasion. For sensational celebrations of the highest calibre, the striking Champagne Bar is the place to be; enjoy fresh oysters with vintage bubbly from a vantage point overlooking the private marina and beyond, watching as the sun sets over the gilded horizon. For exotic cocktails and moreish nibbles, drop into the sizzling Laguna Bar. With such a dazzling array of attractive choices, it is possible to alternate between venues to suit the mood as the evening progresses, culminating with a live music performance at the InMotion nightclub. If heading into central Split for the evening, glamorous motor launch transfers à la James Bond are the most stylish way to make an entrance, launching from the hotel's private yacht marina. But for those who prefer a more sedentary style of leisure, Le Méridien Lav has the perfect alternative.

Sink into a sleek sun lounger, attract the attention of a friendly waiter and soak in the sun next to the stunning outdoor pool. In this seamlessly run hotel, the only dilemma guests will ever face is most likely to be which perfectly chilled cocktail to order next.

PHOTOGRAPHS COURTESY OF LE MÉRIDIEN LAV SPLIT.

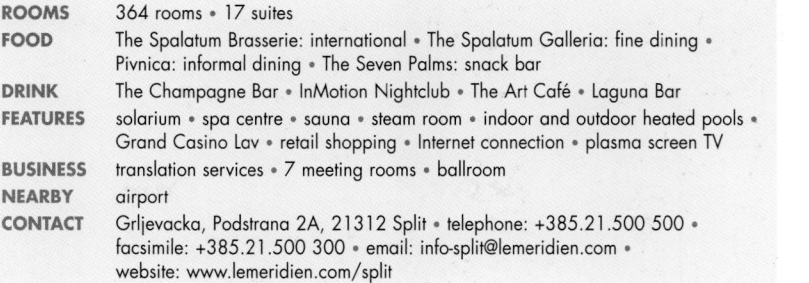

FACTS

ROOMS	364 rooms • 17 suites
FOOD	The Spalatum Brasserie: international • The Spalatum Galleria: fine dining • Pivnica: informal dining • The Seven Palms: snack bar
DRINK	The Champagne Bar • InMotion Nightclub • The Art Café • Laguna Bar
FEATURES	solarium • spa centre • sauna • steam room • indoor and outdoor heated pools • Grand Casino Lav • retail shopping • Internet connection • plasma screen TV
BUSINESS	translation services • 7 meeting rooms • ballroom
NEARBY	airport
CONTACT	Grljevacka, Podstrana 2A, 21312 Split • telephone: +385.21.500 500 • facsimile: +385.21.500 300 • email: info-split@lemeridien.com • website: www.lemeridien.com/split

Hotel Sv Mihovil

Lovers of nature, recreation, the outdoors and adventure will truly have found paradise in the faultlessly located Hotel Sv Mihovil. A core of welcoming, old-fashioned service is fronted by a modern, white-washed façade at the Hotel Sv Mihovil (or St Michael, when anglicised), which boasts two acclaimed restaurants, and an enchanting view of the picturesque River Cetina as well as myriad opportunities for the thrillseeking traveller to experience a wide range of Croatia's most breathtaking adventure sports.

This long-established family-run hotel has an 80-year history and is located by the clear waters of the River Cetina near Trilj, in Dalmatia. It is just 10 minutes from the new highway that has made Croatia's attractions all the more easily accessible, a mere half an hour's drive away from the coastal city and international airport of Split.

The hotel has 28 light and spacious rooms, of which two are luxuriously furnished guest suites. Each air-conditioned room has a direct-dial telephone, satellite television and a well-stocked mini-bar. Most rooms overlook the stunning Cetina River and the nearby archeological site of Tilurij—an ideal venue for a late afternoon stroll.

Sv Mihovil's Čaporice restaurant rates among Croatia's Top 100 eateries, and has been delighting both locals and guests for generations. Its exquisite menu of authentic Cetina dishes showcases all the freshest seasonal produce, including frog, crayfish, arambašići (stuffed cabbage leaves) and cooked lamb in Dalmatian tomato sauce. Recipes remain faithful to their traditional roots, with contemporary culinary updates. Čaporice staff are adept at catering to every dining requirement, from candlelit meals for two on the summer terrace, to gala dinners, ceremonies and corporate events.

The hotel has two cosy cafés. The comfortable Café Sv Mihovil's is just the place to relax with a fresh pastry, a steaming cappuccino and a newspaper, soaking up the sunshine on the terrace. As the sun moves westwards, follow its progress by adjourning to Café Natura. Enjoy a slice of homemade tiramisu in this willow-shaded haven on the banks of the River Cetina.

THIS PAGE (CLOCKWISE FROM TOP): **The Hotel Sv Mihovil offers a range of adventure sports for the active; the riverside Café Natura by the Cetina provides welcome shade in the afternoon, as well as light refreshments throughout the day; white-water rafting is available for the more adventurous guests.**

OPPOSITE: Canoeing is a popular activity of choice for guests at the Hotel Sv Mihovil, as part of its focus on adventure holidays.

...opportunities to experience a range of Croatia's most breathtaking adventure sports.

After such gastronomic indulgences, a visit to the fitness centre will soon help to restore the balance between excess and exercise. Alternatively, take advantage of the many fantastic adventure opportunities available at the Hotel's Avanturist Club. Introduce an active element to any stay with a round of white-water river rafting, horse trekking or an extended canoe safari.

Biking and canyoning opportunities are also available, all carried out in and around the lush green hills of Trilj and the beautiful River Cetina region. The Avanturist Club at the hotel has its own bikes, stables and watersports equipment, and will organise expertly run itineraries of between one and seven days' duration upon request.

Surrounded by fresh air, vineyards, crystal clear springs and brooks, this hidden corner of Croatia has equal measures of serenity and adrenaline for those looking for either. Experience it all alongside first-class, friendly service at the Hotel Sv Mihovil.

PHOTOGRAPHS COURTESY OF HOTEL SV MIHOVIL.

FACTS

ROOMS	26 rooms • 2 luxury suites
FOOD	Restaurant Čaporice: local
DRINK	Café Sv Mihovil • Café Natura
FEATURES	direct-dial telephone • air-conditioning • satellite TV • mini-bar •
SERVICES	conference hall for up to 50 delegates • fitness centre • Avanturist Club (canoeing, kayaking, mountain bike tours, rafting, horse riding)
NEARBY	Trilj • Split • international airport
CONTACT	Ul Bana Jelačića 8, 21240 Trilj • telephone: +385.21.831 790 • facsimile: +385.21.831 770 • email: sv.mihovil@inet.hr • website: www.svmihovil.com

Adriana, hvar marina hotel and spa

THIS PAGE: *The harbour of Hvar is always a sight to behold, taking in spectacular views of the sea.*

OPPOSITE (FROM TOP): *Lavender fields nearby perfume the air, bringing a soft edge to the island breeze; specialist massage is only one of the many body treatments and programmes at the Adriana.*

During the Cold War and the subsequent break-up of the former Yugoslavia, Croatia was effectively cut off from the rest of the world, yet a few still managed to hear many wonderful things about the country. They heard about the crystal clear waters of its seas, and the miles of empty white pebble beaches. They heard tales of its amazing, near-perfect Mediterranean climate, filled with long sunny days and pleasantly cool nights. They heard about its friendly people, and the varied culinary influences which had shaped the local cuisine. They heard about its beautiful landscapes, glorious medieval architecture and many historic villages and towns—a treasure trove full of discoveries waiting for that first intrepid visitor.

But there was one point on which the perennially buzzing travel grapevine seemed to remain distressingly silent: the availability

of reputable places to stay, places that would live up to high global expectations of style, service and comfort. In short, places that offered all the benefits of a new and unspoilt destination combined with all the amenities of an older, more established one. The reason that they never heard of such places was that they simply didn't exist, and when Croatia finally opened up to tourists a few years ago, many were reluctant to make the commitment of spending a holiday there.

Such concerns, however, are no longer justified. Croatia has adapted rapidly—it has advanced far beyond all recognition—and nowhere else is this more apparent than on the country's Dalmatian coast. Here, cutting-edge architecture and design have been blended with the highest possible standards of both customer service and satisfaction to create some of Europe's most stunning new hotels, transforming Croatia into the true world-class holiday destination that it has always deserved to be.

There is no better example of this kind of fresh and exciting development than the brand-new Adriana, hvar marina hotel and spa, which, along with its sister hotel, the nearby Riva, hvar yacht harbor hotel, has led the way in redefining the parameters of style and comfort that now characterise the 'new look' of the Dalmatian coast.

Located right on the Hvar waterfront, overlooking the seaside promenade, the Adriana offers spectacular views of the old city centre, including the Cathedral, The Arsenal and one of the biggest Venetian piazzas in the region. Beyond the intricate tapestry of old town and new development, the lush hills act as a beautiful backdrop to the cityscape set below. One of the best ways to enjoy these views is from the roof terrace, where a heated saltwater pool, gleaming sky bar and lounge area alternate between open-air chill-out zone and sheltered retreat, courtesy of a sleek retractable canopy that enables the terrace to accommodate guests despite the vagaries of the weather. Here guests can indulge in a swim, a therapeutic massage or a poolside drink in the soothing surrounds of this most relaxing of holiday environments.

There is another bar in the hotel lobby, and a restaurant with its own terrace that specialises in serving up fish and seafood prepared in a variety of Mediterranean styles. All of the dishes on the menu are prepared to the very highest international standards by talented chefs using carefully selected and locally sourced ingredients.

The Adriana offers guests a choice of 54 guestrooms and eight suites, all of which come with air-conditioning, wireless Internet access, satellite television and a private balcony or terrace. Without doubt, however, the highlight of any stay at the Adriana is its evocatively named in-house Sensori Spa, inspired by a luxuriance of all that one can

see, hear, touch, taste and smell. This exquisitely appointed spa complex stretches across four levels, integrating culturally local design elements with those of the most sophisticated international fashions, and comes fully equipped to cater for even the most jaded doyennes of spa connoisseurs.

As the name implies, the Sensori Spa celebrates the senses, offering a sumptuous spa experience that transcends both time and culture. Here, the emphasis is firmly on intelligent healing programmes and therapies that balance and synchronise the body and the mind as well as the spirit. Treatments at

the Sensori Spa draw upon a diverse variety of contemporary spa techniques and recent technologies, indigenous herbaceous flora and traditional local folk remedies, not to mention the invigorating qualities of the sea, air and land of Hvar island itself.

Amongst the many features that the spa has to offer guests are a movement studio with programmes for yoga and meditation, four massage parlours with a wide choice of different massage styles, two facial massage rooms, the signature Sensori bath ritual, and three wet treatment rooms. Any one of these programmes is personally guaranteed by the

spa's experienced therapists to fully relax and thoroughly rejuvenate every single spa visitor both mentally and physically.

Last, but by no means least, the Adriana, hvar marina hotel and spa offers its guests the opportunity to experience the beautiful island of Hvar itself. Leisure opportunities include sightseeing in the surrounding little town, with its enchanting mosaic of shops, pavement cafés, monastery and historic fortresses. Not to mention that just a short boat ride away, there are plenty of lovely islands and white beaches to explore. Hiking and scuba diving possibilities also abound here, as does the chance to soak up the variegated atmosphere of this charming island, its culture and also its people.

Croatia may have been overlooked by visitors in the past, but things have definitely changed, and if the Adriana, hvar marina hotel and spa and its sister hotel the Riva are any indication to go by, it's certain to get a lot more global attention in the future.

FACTS	**ROOMS**	54 rooms • 8 suites
	FOOD	Mediterranean seafood restaurant • 24-hour room service
	DRINK	Lobby Bar • Sky Bar and Lounge • sundeck lounge
	FEATURES	rooftop indoor/outdoor pool • Sensori Spa • wireless Internet connection • disabled access • pet-friendly
	BUSINESS	2 meeting rooms • 24-hour business services • office equipment rental
	NEARBY	Paklinski Islands • scuba diving • jet skiing • parasailing • Humac Eco Village • Franciscan monastery • Spanish fortress
	CONTACT	21450 Hvar • telephone: +385.21.750 750 • facsimile: +385.21.750 751 • email: reservations@suncanihvar.com • website: www.suncanihvar.com

PHOTOGRAPHS COURTESY OF SUNCANI HVAR HOTELS.

Riva, hvar yacht harbor hotel

Throughout much of the last century, much of Croatia's international reputation centred around two things. The first was as a place of tremendous natural beauty, unspoilt towns and villages, secluded coves and empty white pebble beaches, interesting cuisines and friendly people. The second was for the political unrest that troubled the country, effectively cutting it off from the rest of the world. The two effectively cancelled each other out, with the result that few people ever dared venture there. But thanks to the recent political developments that have taken place, all that has changed now, and for the first time in its history travellers from all over the world are able to discover Croatia's merits as a tourist destination for themselves.

THIS PAGE (FROM LEFT): A dramatic sunset over Hvar marks the start of yet another glamorous night at Riva, the island's chic hotspot; sleek, modern lines and effortless style typify interior spaces of the Riva, hvar yacht harbor hotel.

OPPOSITE: The Riva's waterfront promenade glows in the evening light as boats rest in their berths after a fulfilling day of sailing.

Of course, there has been a lot of catching up to do—the leap from idyllic unspoilt backwater to major tourist hotspot does not happen overnight. But due to some thoughtful investment and hard work Croatia is now able to offer world-class facilities and levels of service that were previously unheard of in the country, and one fine example of this can be found on the island of Hvar on the beautiful Dalmatian coast.

The Riva, hvar yacht harbor hotel is Croatia's first and only member of the highly respected Small Luxury Hotels of the World group, and it is no exaggeration to say that it has, along with its nearby sister hotel the new Adriana, hvar marina hotel and spa, transformed the region's ability to cater for even the most discerning travellers, no matter how high their holiday expectations.

...the best of both worlds—old-world charm and sophisticated luxury.

Overlooking the palm-fringed waterfront promenade at the heart of the picturesque little town of Hvar, this recently renovated 100-year-old building melds the best of both worlds—old-world charm and sophisticated luxury. With 53 uniquely designed rooms, all of them furnished and decorated to the highest of any contemporary standards, the Riva, hvar yacht harbor hotel sets a new benchmark for levels of service and satisfaction that hitherto had only been found in such established coastal retreats as the Amalfi coast of Italy and the south of France.

Among the attractive features of this hotel is its restaurant, Roots. A lot of thought has gone into providing guests with a dining experience that combines the best traditional Mediterranean dishes with culinary styles from around the world, put together with the finest and freshest local ingredients. After dinner, guests can relax to the music of well-known DJs in Hvar's hottest bar, the BB club. Located on a spacious outdoor terrace and set against a backdrop of luxury yachts, there is no better place to spend an evening, and it's no wonder that it has become something of a landmark in Hvar's summer scene.

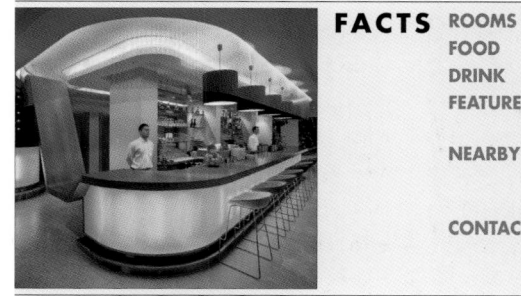

FACTS

ROOMS	45 rooms • 8 suites
FOOD	Roots restaurant: Mediterranean
DRINK	BB club
FEATURES	yacht marina • disabled access • massage room • wireless Internet connection • pet-friendly
NEARBY	Paklinski Islands • The Arsenal • Hvar Theatre • Franciscan monastery • Spanish fortress • Napoleon's fortress • Humac Eco Village • parasailing • scuba diving • jet skiing
CONTACT	21450 Hvar • telephone: +385.21.750 750 • facsimile: +385.21.750 751 • email: reservations@suncanihvar.com • website: www.suncanihvar.com

Palmizana Meneghello

Everyone sometimes dreams of escaping to a tropical island paradise—to places a million miles away from our workaday lives where we can indulge our every whim. For some, this is no more than an idle daydream, impossible in reality. To others, it's a perfectly realisable goal thanks to the existence of places such as Palmizana, a small island off the coast of Hvar in the southern Adriatic.

The Venetian Meneghello family first settled the island in the 1700s. Over the years they transformed it into the arcadian paradise it is today—a bohemian Garden of Eden set in 300 hectares (741 acres) of

THIS PAGE (FROM RIGHT): A cheerful nook in one of the bungalows; the Restaurant Palmizana is well-known regionally for its exquisite fresh seafood dishes; minimalist décor has no place at the Meneghello, where bright colours energise the atmosphere.

OPPOSITE: The cosy living area in the Villa White comfortably accommodates up to six people for those lazy afternoon chats.

uninhabited virgin territory complete with a protected nature reserve, an exotic botanical park, private beaches and some of the clearest, cleanest waters in the world.

But while the idea of 'getting back to nature' is one of the foremost attractions of any stay on the island, life's little luxuries have not been overlooked. In 1999, the resort was refurbished to the highest modern standards. Today, guests find themselves in a world where troubles are soon forgotten and

complete relaxation is all but guaranteed. There are 16 different accommodation units to choose from, ranging from bungalows and villas to houses and apartments. Sleeping between two and 10 people, all are distinct from each other, thoughtfully furnished, close to the water's edge and enjoy stunning views in every direction.

It's a boat ride to the nearest town, but guests at Palmizana needn't go far for one of the finest restaurants around. With recipes and skills passed down through generations of the Meneghello family, the resort's chefs prepare cuisine based on locally sourced ingredients, all served on a beautiful seaside terrace decorated with driftwood sculptures. Fresh seafood comes straight from the fisherman's net, and organic greens from the island's gardens. The result is a glimpse of gastronomic heaven and it's no surprise that yachtsmen from all over the Adriatic make regular use of the 200-berth marina while stopping by for an unparalleled meal.

There's no shortage of activities either. The diving here is excellent—the surrounding waters are crystal clear and teeming with life, coral reefs and ancient shipwrecks. Deep-sea fishing and pheasant shooting provide other options, and sailing, water-skiing and windsurfing can all be easily arranged. There's also an art gallery nearby, and the botanical garden, created in 1906, has one of the finest collections of exotic plants in Croatia, including various agaves, mimosas, laurels and the many aromatic herbs for which the island has become famous. For most people though, there's nothing to beat taking a long walk along the deserted beachfront, soaking up the vivid silence and losing themselves in the sheer beauty of the natural world around them.

FACTS

ROOMS	5 bungalows • 5 villas • 6 apartments
FOOD	Restaurant Palmizana: seafood and continental
DRINK	Toto's bar
FEATURES	nature reserve • botanical garden • private beaches • 200-berth marina • art gallery • pet-friendly
NEARBY	Hvar • sea sports centre • boat rental service • pheasant hunting (fall and winter)
CONTACT	Meneghello Estate, Palmizana, 21450 Hvar • telephone: +385.21.717 270 • facsimile: +385.21.717 268 • email: palmizana@palmizana.hr • website: www.palmizana.hr

PHOTOGRAPHS COURTESY OF PALMIZANA MENEGHELLO.

Hotel Šipan

The citizens of Dubrovnik should know a thing or two about holiday destinations. After all, they live in one. For this reason, it's interesting to note that when they want to 'get away from it all' they have for centuries favoured the little-known but delightful island of Šipan in the southern Adriatic, just 14.5 km (9 miles) from the city.

The main reason for Šipan's enduring appeal is not just its natural beauty, but also the fact that it has remained completely unspoiled and untouched by modern developments. Only 9.7 km (6 miles) long and 3.2 km (2 miles) wide with a population of 500, it's a pristine wilderness where visitors can quickly lose themselves in nature and escape from all the hustle and bustle of the real world just over the horizon.

There's only one place to stay, the Hotel Šipan in the seaside village of Šipanska Luka, formerly an olive factory that was converted into the hotel that it is today in 1979 and completely renovated in 2006. Situated close to the water's edge and at the head of a long, narrow bay, the hotel offers magnificent views over both land and sea and the kind of peace and tranquillity that only small islands such as Šipan can offer.

The hotel has 83 rooms and four suites, as well as a luxury apartment situated in a 100-year-old stone villa. All rooms have en suite bathrooms, and are tastefully decorated

and furnished throughout with traditional pieces to give them a cosy, warm feel of total comfort and relaxation.

The Pjat Restaurant is rightly a source of pride to the hotel staff. Located in a stone villa redolent with history, it offers creative Mediterranean cuisine with exotic influences prepared by a dedicated and talented team of chefs. Local ingredients are used where possible and meals are served with a choice of the finest Croatian and international wines

THIS PAGE (FROM TOP): The newly refurbished rooms exude calm in shades of nude and earth; bathrooms are sleekly outfitted, brightly lit and fully stocked with hotel amenities and toiletries.

OPPOSITE (CLOCKWISE FROM LEFT): An enchanting view of the hotel; the waterfront grounds of the hotel glow softly in the dusk light coming in from the bay; hotel diners can enjoy gourmet Mediterranean cuisine and wine at the excellent Restaurant Pjat.

from the hotel's impressive cellar. On the waterfront, the attractive BarKa Cocktail Bar & Café serves breakfasts in the morning, coffee, ice cream, snacks and afternoon tea later in the day, and transforms seamlessly into a delightful wine bar in the evenings. The hotel has facilities to cater for up to 80 people in their fully equipped conference centre, making it an ideal place to hold a business meeting or other social event, such as a wedding or anniversary party.

That said, the undisputed star of the whole holiday experience at the Hotel Šipan is without doubt the island itself, and for those who might have spent an afternoon hiking in the exuberantly rugged countryside surrounding the hotel, or swimming, fishing, or indulging in a spot of diving in the island's crystal clear waters, the hotel also offers a temptingly wide range of relaxing massages and aromatherapy treatments, making for the perfect end to a day in paradise.

FACTS

ROOMS	83 rooms • 4 suites • 1 apartment
FOOD	Restaurant Pjat: Mediterranean fusion
DRINK	BarKa Cocktail Bar & Café • wine cellar
FEATURES	massage • aromatherapy • scuba diving • yacht mooring
BUSINESS	conference centre
NEARBY	Šipan • Skocibuha Castle • beaches • Elaphiti Archipelago • Dubrovnik
CONTACT	Šipanska Luka 160, 20223 Šipanska Luka, Otok Šipan, Dubrovnik • telephone: +385.20.758 000 • facsimile: +385.20.758 004 • email: hotel-sipan@petral.hr • website: www.hotel-sipan.com

PHOTOGRAPHS COURTESY OF HOTEL ŠIPAN.

Hotel Glavovic

destination for families and couples alike, its welcoming locals are always ready to embrace visitors and initiate them into the famed customs of hospitality the island is known for. It is renowned for its rich Mediterranean flora and the fine white sands of Sunj beach. Pronounced 'Shoon', this is reputedly the most beautiful beach in all of the Elafiti islands. A brief stroll from the hotel, the beach is best enjoyed on a quiet day in order to experience the cobalt blue waters of the Adriatic at their very best.

Run by gregarious hosts Luka and Vlasta, the hotel is a comfortable blend of genuine hospitality and stylish waterfront accommodation. Its central position offers easy access to the island's wide selection of

THIS PAGE (FROM TOP): The Hotel Glavovic is located along the waterfront promenade of Lopud, one of the lovely Elafiti islands; the constant coming and going along the promenade provides for guests who enjoy people-watching over a cup of coffee.

OPPOSITE (FROM LEFT): The white sandy beach is one source of pleasure for visitors to Lopud; small motor boats like this are convenient for offshore forays.

Hotel Glavovic is one of the rare three-star hotels on the island of Lopud. Completely renovated in 2004, this imposing stone building occupies a picturesque location at the heart of the horseshoe-shaped bay on the island's southwest coast. Dating back to 1927, it stands as the oldest family-run hotel on the colourful waterfront promenade, and indeed on the whole island.

An oasis of peace and tranquillity, the car-free island of Lopud is just a 40-minute ferry ride away from Dubrovnik. An ideal

Hotel Glavovic has 12 bright, airy and comfortable guestrooms and two larger apartments. Each room is individually air-conditioned and features satellite TV and radio, Internet connection and a dedicated telephone extension. The panoramic views from the private balconies and sea-facing suites are a particular highlight of each stay. They extend out over the patchwork of warm vermillion rooftops, past the gaily bobbing sailboats, taking in dramatically sweeping views of the island-speckled Adriatic.

The hotel's traditional restaurant has one of the best and longest established culinary reputations on an island with its fair share of eateries and restaurants. In its comfortable and laid-back dining room, or indeed out on the cooling quayside balcony, hotel guests and town residents alike enjoy a choice selection of freshly grilled fish and shellfish, succulent cuts of meats paired with vegetarian platters. A quaintly aged piano lends an air of old-time authenticity to the restaurant, its

walls dotted with charming little oil-paintings from the 1930s and homey photographs straight out of the family album.

With a diverse menu of activities that ranges from leisurely sea-kayaking to beach volleyball, diving and fishing, Lopud offers something for each and every different taste. Visitors who want a break from the mainland and the mainstream can do so here by indulging in a spot of island-living at the versatile and welcoming Hotel Glavovic.

bars, restaurants and beaches. The hosts will happily arrange tours to Lopud's numerous cultural attractions, which include two monasteries, a museum, upwards of thirty chapels and the historic remains of many sites of religious significance. If pressed for time, the Rector's Palace and Spanish Fort in particular are well worth a visit.

PHOTOGRAPHS COURTESY OF HOTEL GLAVOVIC.

FACTS		
ROOMS	12 rooms • 2 apartments	
FOOD	Restaurant Glavovic: local	
DRINK	wine list	
FEATURES	satellite TV • radio • Internet connection	
SERVICES	fax and Internet facilities at reception	
NEARBY	botanical gardens • Sunj Beach • Spanish Fort • Rector's Palace • tennis • outdoor pool	
CONTACT	Obala Ivana Kuljevana, 20222 Lopud • telephone: +385.20.759 359 • facsimile: +385.20.759 358 • email: info@hotel-glavovic.hr • website: www.hotel-glavovic.hr	

Hilton Imperial Dubrovnik

Picturesque views of bright fairytale turrets, mountain spires and glittering misty islands are never far away in Dubrovnik. In the midst of this enchanting landscape is the Hilton Imperial Dubrovnik, the resort of choice for those discerning travellers in search of a luxurious holiday in beautiful surroundings.

Situated mere minutes from the historic Old Town section of Dubrovnik (a UNESCO World Heritage Site) and set amongst its monuments, ancient fort and city walls which date from the 7th to 15th centuries, this grand dame of hotels rises imposingly from the surrounding palm trees, luminous against the night sky. In the day, the hotel's naturally lit indoor pool is a beautiful focal point and a work of art in itself. Sunlight refracts through a glass ceiling that spreads over the length and breadth of the pool, illuminating the interior of the pool house before breaking on the pool's surface in facets of shattered light. Guests inspired by the views from the hotel's intricate balcony, a feature of the original hotel structure which has been lovingly preserved and restored, can explore the idyllic coastline or plunge into the cerulean blue of the Adriatic's sun-kissed waters.

There are several fine restaurants and bars in Dubrovnik's Old Town, but for an authentic Croatian culinary treat, head straight for the hotel's Porat Restaurant. Set in the middle of a charmingly spacious terrace that commands prime views of the town, the restaurant is highly popular with guests and

THIS PAGE (FROM TOP): The grand façade of the Hilton Imperial Dubrovnik, fanned by palms; the luxuriously appointed rooms wait invitingly for the traveller after a long day of leisure.

OPPOSITE: A beautiful night view overlooking Dubrovnik city, from the hotel's terrace where guests can enjoy a romantic evening.

locals alike, some of whom swear by Porat's signature Adriatic sea bass, accompanied by a glass of fruity Dalmatian wine. Post-prandials are best enjoyed in The Bar, a softly lit space furnished in Mediterranean style that serves light refreshment against a quiet backdrop of live music.

When the allure of surfeited fine wining and dining has worn off, the gym and spa beckon. The gym is state of the art, satisfying even the most demanding guests, while the Beauty Line Spa offers luxurious treatments.

Each spacious guestroom incorporates the colours of the city, a blend of bright terracotta, stone and ochre. The impressive views take in the intricate city, the verdant gardens and the nearby mountains. Interiors champion traditional motifs, with local designs and handcrafted wooden furniture. This provides a soothing environment in which to work, surf the high-speed Internet or simply relax in a fluffy bathrobe after the decadence of polished marble bathrooms.

The Hilton Imperial Dubrovnik is not only an ideal holidaymaker's hotel, it is also a favourite of business travellers. High-flying corporate clients will find much to like in the hotel's meeting rooms, executive lounge and business centre. So on account of business, pleasure, or both, the majestic Hilton Imperial in the heart of Dubrovnik is sure to satisfy.

FACTS		
	ROOMS	147 rooms
	FOOD	The Porat Restaurant: local and international
	DRINK	The Bar
	FEATURES	fitness centre • Beauty Line Spa • indoor pool • massage • sauna • wireless Internet connection
	BUSINESS	business centre • 7 meeting rooms • ballroom • executive lounge
	NEARBY	Cilipi International Airport • Old Walled Town
	CONTACT	Marijana Blazica 2, 20000 Dubrovnik • telephone: +385.20.320 320 • facsimile: +385.20.320 220 • email: sales.dubrovnik@hilton.com • website: www.dubrovnik.hilton.com

PHOTOGRAPHS COURTESY OF HILTON IMPERIAL DUBROVNIK.

Hotel Bellevue

The captivating view from the lobby embraces a mountainside monastery surrounded by the cobalt of the Adriatic. This superb view is not incidental but carefully considered, in a hotel where every single element right down to the artwork in the reception area—a specially commissioned piece by Croatia's leading sculptor Dusan Dzamonja—has been meticulously planned to ensure a flawless visit for Dubrovnik's most discerning and affluent visitors.

Visualising a new breed of hotel, designer Renata Strok explains her concept for the Bellevue as being a living process of near-organic evolution, eschewing the gimmicky shine and gloss of many modern hotels and focusing instead on themes of natural serenity. True to these basic tenets, the internal colour palette is informed by rich olive wood, charcoal-hued granite and other matte stone surfaces. All other materials used

The latest striking addition to the Adriatic Luxury Hotels group portfolio of quality travel accommodation is none other than the recently completely refurbished Bellevue Hotel in the historic city of Dubrovnik. Dramatically located on a cliff top, high above the secluded Miramare Bay, this exclusive five-star property scheduled to burst onto the global scene in early 2007 is already causing quite a stir in this most vibrantly enchanting of Mediterranean cities among the well-heeled glitterati.

THIS PAGE (FROM TOP): The full-height glass windows provide guests with a clear view over the city; the guestrooms are havens of luxury, many crowned with an unparalleled view of the water.

OPPOSITE: The Hotel Bellevue is clad throughout in earthy hues, a template of natural materials interspersed with greenery that emphasises the lovely sea view.

complement these tones and tactile textures, and the uninterrupted sea views from the Bellevue's welcoming lobby round off this harmonious aesthetic experience.

Co-existing as a counter-foil to the Dubrovnik Palace—its multi-award-winning sister hotel—the Bellevue has already created its own niche. It appeals to the new breed of young and dynamic leisure travellers who recognise good stylistic company whenever and wherever they see it, and who prefer to avoid the homogeneity of faceless, branded properties at all costs.

The 80 climate-controlled rooms and 13 suites are stylishly understated. The minimalist wooden floors and sleek furnishings rival the gleaming super yachts that glide in and out of view from the private balconies in 'chic factor' rating. And though themes of nature are prevalent as a design leitmotif, the Bellevue knows full well that a little cutting-edge technology never did anyone any harm. The suites boast 'smart-room' technology with Interactive TV and Internet access, to make every stay as pleasurable and memorable as possible. A cinema, fitness centre, magnificent indoor pool and extensive spa facilities are only a select few out of the list of modern comforts inconspicuously tucked away amongst the hotel's many conveniences and amenities.

When the time comes to heed the inviting call of gustatory delights, dine in the hotel's first-class restaurant or sip a chilled glass of local white wine at the private beach's sea-level bar. Those headed into town will also revel in Dubrovnik's many acclaimed restaurants and bars.

With all the beauty of nature's finest seascapes for dreamy escapists or nights out in Dubrovnik's lively old Walled Town for connoisseurs of heady draughts of joie de vivre, the perfectly located Bellevue succeeds in the oft-aspired to yet rarely attained melding of the best of both worlds.

FACTS		
	ROOMS	80 rooms • 12 suites • 1 presidential suite
	FOOD	À La Carte Restaurant • Spice Lounge • Beach Tavern
	DRINK	Beach Bar
	FEATURES	Interactive TV • Internet connection • mini-bar • dedicated telephone lines • jacuzzi (suites only) • cinema • spa and wellness centre • indoor pool • fitness club • sauna • hair salon • shops • private beach
	NEARBY	international airport • Dubrovnik's Old Town
	CONTACT	Pera Cingrije 7, 20000 Dubrovnik • telephone: +385.20.330 000 • facsimile: +385.20.330 100 • email: welcome@hotel-bellevue.hr • website: www.hotel-bellevue.hr

PHOTOGRAPHS COURTESY OF ADRIATIC LUXURY HOTELS.

Hotel Dubrovnik Palace

The search for 'Croatia's Leading Hotel' and 'Croatia's Leading Spa Resort' is over at last. The Hotel Dubrovnik Palace is the proud new holder of these two highly sought-after World Travel Awards accolades.

A bird's-eye perspective of the Hotel Dubrovnik Palace reveals the resort as a city unto itself, cradled on the one side by crystal blue Adriatic waters and by aromatic pine forests on the other, with panoramic views of the Elafiti Islands scattered off the shores of the beautiful Lapad Peninsula. The hotel is the vision of Croatian painter and acclaimed interior designer Renata Strok, tantamount to

an enormous art gallery that seamlessly showcases Croatia's vast pool of highly original artistic talent. This sanctuary has an air of timeless simplicity that instantly puts guests at ease with its unpretentious beauty.

An ideal evening of culinary chic in Dubrovnik starts off with sipping a perfectly chilled twilight aperitif at the water's edge in Maslina Tavern, followed by an intimate dinner at Lenga, where the highly celebrated mango and mussel soup with ginger shrimp quenelles and the pepper seared yellow fin tuna carpaccio with basil champagne sorbet are irresistible house specialities.

The hotel's cascading style of architecture means that each of the 308 rooms and suites boasts individual private balconies and sea views. The interior design features natural materials such as polished wood and stone interspersed with vivid flashes of colour from contemporary art and fresh flowers. Rooms come with the latest high-tech gadgetry: flat-screen satellite TV and high-speed wireless Internet. Bathrooms are decadently stocked up with exclusive Gharani Strok toiletries.

Fitness buffs and spa enthusiasts will adore the Wren's Club spa and fitness centre, where core training programmes such as yoga and pilates are available. A must-visit for honeymooners is the couples' treatment room offering luxurious treats such as hot stone massage and seaweed wraps.

With some of the best diving in Europe to be found in Adriatic waters, the Palace's Dive Centre will be first port of call for sub-aqua enthusiasts. For beginners, Discovery Dives are the ideal starting point, while the less adventurous are welcome to take advantage of the heated indoor pool or one of three outdoor pools delicately nestled in the meticulously manicured gardens.

The Old City of Dubrovnik is minutes away from the hotel grounds, making city exploration a matter of conveniently hopping on a bus or taxi. In the summer months a boat goes directly between the hotel's private quay and the old port. However, with all that it has to offer, guests may ultimately find it difficult to tear themselves away from the treats and comforts of the Hotel Dubrovnik Palace.

THIS PAGE (FROM LEFT): Rooms at the Hotel Dubrovnik Palace are statements of modern chic; the Orlandinjo Club is the place to go for stylish cocktails and live jazz in the cool evenings.

OPPOSITE (FROM TOP): Sea views and exquisitely prepared cuisine vie with each other for attention; one of the hotel's four beautiful pools where guests can spend a relaxing and leisurely afternoon.

FACTS

ROOMS	270 rooms • 36 suites • 1 presidential suite
FOOD	Elafiti: international • Lenga: local fine dining • Tavern Maslina: informal dining
DRINK	Lanterna Glorijet • Oazarium • Orlandinjo Club • Sunset Lounge • Vala Bara
FEATURES	PADI dive centre • Wren's Spa and Health Club • indoor pool • 3 outdoor pools • tennis court • hair salon • shop gallery • beach • disabled access
BUSINESS	conference centre • 10 multi-functional meeting rooms
NEARBY	airport • Old City • Mljet • Korcula
CONTACT	Masarykov put 20, 20000 Dubrovnik • telephone: +385.20.430 000 • facsimile: +385.20.430 100 • email: info@dubrovnikpalace.hr • website: www.dubrovnikpalace.hr

Hotel Excelsior

Corporate travellers and tourists alike are drawn all year round to Dubrovnik's sun-drenched walled town, enthralled by its eclectic mix of Venetian art and religious and military architecture from Renaissance and Baroque periods. The discerning visitor's choice from which to enjoy these highlights of the Mediterranean is the Hotel Excelsior of the Adriatic Luxury Hotels group. Hotel Excelsior is one of Croatia's most internationally renowned hotels, a haven of luxury and exclusivity in the very heart of ancient Dubrovnik. A landmark building, it rises majestically out of the city over the enticingly blue waters of the Adriatic.

Leading Croatia's revival as one of the Mediterranean's most stylish destinations, the Hotel Excelsior was completely renovated in 1998. The elegant sun terraces are perfect for soaking up the stunning vistas over city, sea and nearby Lokrum Island. The complex encompasses a private beach, fitness centre and a dazzlingly exclusive wide range of high-end retail boutiques.

The hotel's 154 bedrooms are luxuriously appointed, equipped with state-of-the-art facilities to make the space within as impressive as the rugged coastal panorama outside. Spacious chambers are accented by tasteful furnishings and beautiful

THIS PAGE (FROM LEFT): The beautiful heated indoor pool beckons; an enchantingly beautiful view of the Hotel Excelsior by night.

OPPOSITE (CLOCKWISE FROM LEFT): Rooms are furnished and dressed in clean classic styles; open-air dining comes with its own ever-changing décor; the breathtaking blue of the Adriatic is the perfect backdrop to the perfect coastal holiday.

...a haven of luxury and exclusivity in the very heart of ancient Dubrovnik.

fabrics, while original paintings by famed Croatian artists grace the walls. Selected rooms have high ceilings and French doors that capture and frame the fantastic gilded sunsets over the Old Town. Individual rooms boast satellite TV, fax machines and Internet connections. The 18 suites have a jacuzzi each, to relax and invigorate after a long day spent either in the streets of Dubrovnik or in business meetings. The hotel is popular with corporate guests for its flawlessly hosted conferences and exhibitions.

Refreshed and ready for dinner, gourmands will love the contemporary chic of Zagreb Restaurant. Its vast terrace is the ideal spot from which to people watch or simply be hypnotised by the timeless lapping of the azure waters of the Adriatic. The Tavern Rustica has a more intimate feel, with an innovative Dalmatian and international menu and an extensive wine list.

The Excelsior's leisure and fitness facilities are second to none. Salon Estetika is designed for pampering and toning the body while remaining enfolded in the lap of luxury. The large, freshwater indoor pool has an entrance out onto the pristine private beach, where those seeking adventure on or beneath the surface of the Adriatic can take their pick of activities—canoe hire, boat trips and scuba diving are popular choices— such is the advantage of the hotel's premium beachside location. Without a doubt, the Hotel Excelsior is truly the embodiment of the coastal holiday experience.

FACTS		
	ROOMS	154 rooms • 18 suites
	FOOD	Restaurant Zagreb: local and international • Tavern Rustica: Dalmatian
	DRINK	Piano Bar • Palm Terrace
	FEATURES	Internet connection • satellite TV • jacuzzi (suites only) • heated indoor pool • private beach • sports facilities
	BUSINESS	5 state-of-the-art meeting rooms • business centre
	NEARBY	Cilipi International Airport
	CONTACT	Frana Supila 12, 20000 Dubrovnik • telephone: +385.20.353 353 • facsimile: +385.20.353 555 • email: info@hotel-excelsior.hr • website: www.hotel-excelsior.hr

The Pucic Palace

Despite stiff competition from neighbouring towns and cities for the title, few could or would challenge the fact that, by common consensus, Dubrovnik is unofficially referred to as 'the jewel of the Adriatic'. A UNESCO World Heritage Site, this medieval walled city epitomises the charm, beauty, vibrance, and cultural richness that the region is known for. And if Dubrovnik is 'the jewel of the Adriatic', then 'the jewel of Dubrovnik' is most certainly The Pucic Palace Hotel.

Situated on Gundulic Square in the heart of the old city, this former nobleman's home and long-time favourite of visiting dignitaries, royalty and artists has recently been completely refurbished and has now re-opened as one of Croatia's finest hotels—a true palace in its most literal sense.

The 19 gloriously furnished rooms and suites at The Pucic Palace skilfully combine stylistic elements of old-world elegance, such as high ceilings held up by dark wood beams, antique furnishings and oak floors, with a range of sophisticated technological features such as satellite television sets, DVD players, wireless Internet access points and air-conditioning. The ultimate result of this blend is as fully sumptuous and polished as it is comfortable and functional.

Lest one think that all this grandeur in the living areas will leave the intimate spaces cramped and fussy, the bathrooms exhibit a scale of opulence that is all their own. With thousands of Romanesque mosaic tiles lining the walls, oversized windows letting in the clear natural light, brightly burnished copper

THIS PAGE (FROM TOP): *Old-world style and elegance is evident throughout the hotel's interiors; lovingly-prepared local cuisine is served daily at the Café Royal.*

OPPOSITE (FROM LEFT): *Wood-beamed ceilings in the guestrooms are a warm addition to the sleek décor; features like sloping ceilings and skylights are incorporated into individual room designs, making each guest's experience unique.*

...one of Croatia's finest hotels—a true palace in its most literal sense.

bathtubs and wash basins, and stocked with luxury lotions and potions fit for an heiress, guests may find it hard to extract themselves from within its pampering confines.

Having said that, with the hotel's three excellent restaurants to choose from, guests might be forgiven if they choose to thoroughly indulge their gustatory senses during their stay at The Pucic Palace. On the ground floor, the Café Royal is a Parisian-style brasserie with outdoor seating on the main square, and serves local specialities including the famous stone soup, which is

flavoured with minerals and pebbles from the Adriatic Sea. The Defne restaurant, by contrast, offers dishes from around the eastern Mediterranean in a more formal setting, with the option of dining outdoors on an open-air terrace. Lastly, there is the Razonoda wine bar, which apart from being Dubrovnik's place-to-be-seen in its capacity as a classy gathering-point for the city's glamorous in-crowd, offers a selection of tasty Croatian finger food, such as local cheeses and hams, as well as a selection of the finest wines, cognacs and cigars.

But no matter how impressive the Pucic Palace is and no matter how tempting it might be to check in and never leave, no stay at the hotel would be complete without taking in the city of Dubrovnik itself. With its cathedrals and castles, its magnificent coastal setting, its quaint cobbled streets and cafés, baroque bell towers and medieval squares, there are more than enough attractions to charm and entertain anyone with any interest in the beauty, history and culture of this fascinating and undiscovered corner of the European continent.

FACTS		
	ROOMS	19 rooms
	FOOD	Café Royal: local • Brasserie Defne: Mediterranean
	DRINK	Razonoda wine bar
	FEATURES	24-hour room service
	NEARBY	Dubrovnik
	CONTACT	Ulica Od Puca 1, 20000 Dubrovnik • telephone: +385.20.326 222 • facsimile: +385.20.326 223 • email: reservations@thepucicpalace.com • website: www.thepucicpalace.com

PHOTOGRAPHS COURTESY OF THE PUCIC PALACE.

Villa Dubrovnik

Selecting a holiday destination can sometimes be a daunting prospect. There are literally thousands of places to choose from and making the right decision is often a hit-and-miss affair, more dependent on luck than judgement. Mistakes are not only costly, but they also create a sense of disappointment that lingers in the memory long after the holiday is over. For this reason, it can be both helpful and comforting to have a well-established and reliable agency

provide a shortlist of properties best suited to individual requirements and therefore more likely to live up to expectations.

The Villa Book is one fine example, a property rental company run by some of the most experienced individuals in the business. Based on a close working relationship with owners and local agents, the staff at The Villa Book take pride in knowing all there is to know about their properties, and in being able to cater for individual requirements, whether it's a romantic getaway you're after, or a larger villa to suit a larger group.

With hundreds of properties on three continents to choose from, the members of staff at The Villa Book are never short of options, and they are particularly strong

THIS PAGE (FROM LEFT): The Villa Dubrovnik rises imposingly over the Dalmatian coast; guests can enjoy refreshments out on the hotel terrace.

OPPOSITE (FROM LEFT): The spacious double rooms of the Villa Dubrovnik are luxuriously and comfortably appointed; the warm and inviting décor extends throughout the villa.

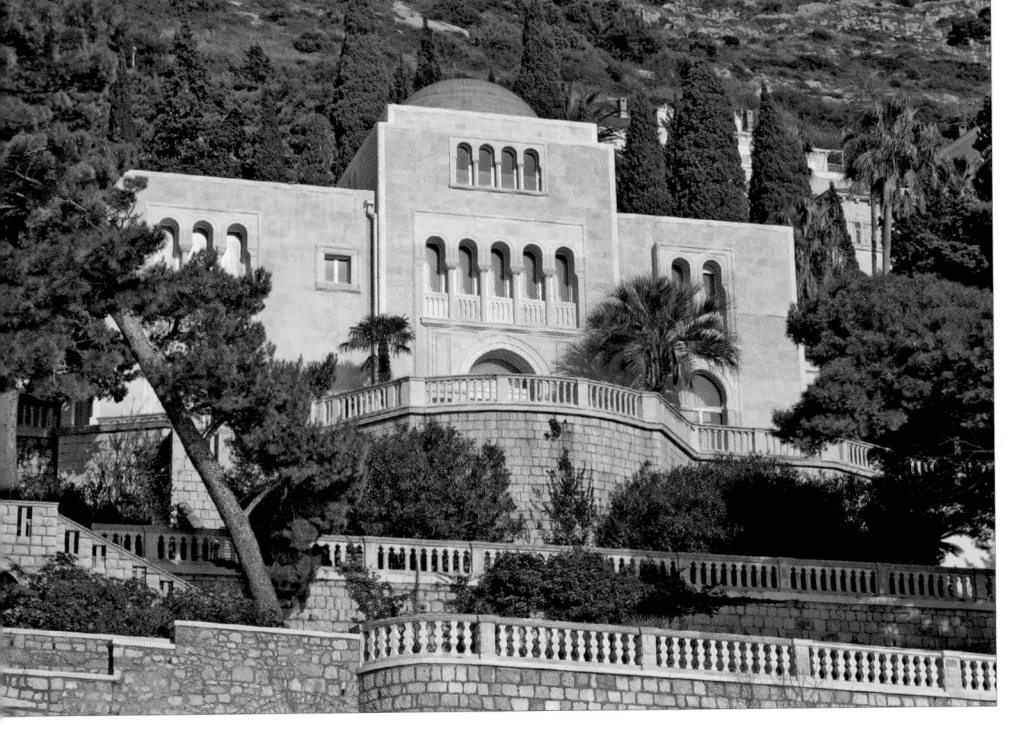

when it comes to destinations on and around the Mediterranean and Adriatic coastlines. Their properties in the region include properties in Italy, Spain, Portugal, France, Morocco, Cyprus, and Croatia.

Villa Dubrovnik is one such property. Located at the southeast end of the beautiful Dalmatian coast just outside the walls of the charming medieval city of the same name, this imposing white stone villa sits within private grounds, where verdant swathes of lush landscaped garden stretch down to a private pier and rocky beach.

The building itself has been recently renovated to a very high standard and consists of five spacious double bedrooms, all of which come with satellite television and a well-stocked mini-bar, besides having a marble en suite bathroom complete with jacuzzi and magnificent views of the Adriatic and the nearby island of Lokrum. With a grand salon and formal gardens that can comfortably receive over 100 seated guests, the luxurious Villa Dubrovnik makes for a perfect venue for wedding receptions and other similar social functions.

Perhaps best of all, Villa Dubrovnik's superb location—a mere few minutes away from Dubrovnik itself—means that guests can enjoy the best of two different worlds. On the one hand, they have all the advantages of the peace and tranquillity of the unspoilt countryside. On the other hand, just a short walk away, they have instant access to one of Europe's most historic cities and all of the delights that it has to offer. Restaurants, museums, churches, theatre and live music—all can be found within its ancient walls of this most fascinating of destinations.

FACTS

ROOMS	5 double rooms
FOOD	full-time cook
DRINK	mini-bar
FEATURES	outdoor pool
NEARBY	Dubrovnik • Adriatic Sea
CONTACT	12 Venetian House, 47 Warrington Crescent, London W9 1EJ • telephone: +44.845.500 2000 • facsimile: +44.845.500 2001 • email: info@thevillabook.com • website: www.thevillabook.com

PHOTOGRAPHS COURTESY OF THE VILLA BOOK.

Dubrovnik House Gallery

The Dubrovnik House Gallery may be likened to an endlessly captivating puzzle box that throws up fascinating new artefacts with each twist and turn. Visitors are known to spend hours browsing its myriad of quirky and unique items only to emerge from the premises wondering where the time went.

Snug within the walls of a 14th-century tower, the gallery is a vital element of the World Heritage city of Dubrovnik, a part of its old city walls, alive with culture and tradition. Dubrovnik House displays the art,

crafts, wines and foods of Croatia to great effect, shunning the bare minimalism of most contemporary galleries for the organic look and feel of wood and stone.

The ground floor houses a well-stocked wine cellar, celebrating the area's vinicultural history. Local varietals Dingaè, Postup, Plavac and Maraština are the main focus, and tastings are popular and highly attended events. Croatia is a land rich in wild aromatic and medicinal herbs, which lends itself to the production of homemade brandies and herb liqueurs. Visitors often leave with a bottle or two as souvenirs to be enjoyed long after the holiday is over.

Food lovers will adore the selection of comestibles. The fine local virgin olive oils inspire instant customer loyalty, and there is equally high demand for honey products and marmalades, as well as the array of local sweets—Mediterranean candied fruits, figs

THIS PAGE (FROM TOP): Dubrovnik House Gallery eschews chrome and glass décor, displaying art in warm and welcoming rooms; the gallery's extensive range of wares includes local produce such as honey and fruit confit.

OPPOSITE (FROM LEFT): Three floors of Croatian arts and crafts form a distinctive cultural experience; Dubrovnik House Gallery is an enthusiastic supporter of local artists and their creative work.

by Croatian culture. A short climb upstairs is the *haut niveau* of Croatia's art world. Reserved for the cream of its creative talent, it hosts permanent and travelling exhibits, often attended by the artist in person.

The Gallery's successful attempts in translating history and tradition into modern objects for daily use has achieved critical acclaim, and recently received the Croatian Tourist Board's star award—the Plavi Cvijet—for its sterling efforts. Dubrovnik House is a fascinating repository of the centuries of Croatia's cultural fabric, and, as most visitors have discovered, a full appreciation of what it has to offer is an experience that should always be savoured and never rushed.

and almonds. They sit demurely in gift boxes and displays, exuding an irresistible lure that draws those with a fondness for toothsome treats. The aromatic corner adds to the sensory delight with its fragrant and colourful rows of herb soaps, shampoos and essential oils—a rare visual and olfactory treat.

The second floor claims the realm of aesthetics, displaying the creations of local artists as well as handmade souvenirs inspired

PHOTOGRAPHS COURTESY OF DUBROVNIK HOUSE GALLERY.

FACTS

PRODUCTS	wines • liqueurs • sweets • local produce • local craft • artwork • souvenirs	
FEATURES	art gallery • exhibitions • wine tasting (subject to scheduling) • cultural event calendar	
NEARBY	all attractions in Dubrovnik's Old Town	
CONTACT	Svetog Dominika 2, 20000 Dubrovnik • telephone: +385.20.322 092 • facsimile: +385.20.322 091 • email: ars.longa@du.t-com.hr	

Jewellery Gallery Đardin

Over the centuries the city of Dubrovnik has come to be known as the 'Jewel of the Adriatic', and like any well-cut jewel it is its sheer number of exquisitely crafted facets that make it such a thing of beauty. Take one aspect—there's its superb geographical setting on a dramatic stretch of coastline. From another angle—there's its history, one that dates back to the Bronze Age and encompasses influences from the Roman, Ottoman and Austro-Hungarian empires, to name a few. Yet another side—its picture-postcard layout and the vibrant atmosphere of its streets, with its many and varied cafés, restaurants, bars and nightclubs.

With so much to offer the visitor, one particular aspect of the city is often overlooked: its pre-eminence as a shopper's paradise. In particular, Dubrovnik boasts some of the most skilful artisans and craftsmen in Europe; a prowess that dates back to its heyday as one of the continent's major trading centres; and the results of their expert labour can be readily found in the city if one knows where to look.

One such place is the Jewellery Gallery Đardin, set in the sublime surroundings of an enclosed garden (Đardin means 'garden' in the local dialect) on Miha Pracata in the heart of the old city. Under the holding name Cro Art Design, the gallery has one of the largest selections of necklaces, bracelets, rings, earrings and other accessories on offer in the region, all designed and manufactured by hand under the guidance of the locally acclaimed duo of Mihovil Ritonija and Margareta Juzvisen-Margo.

Having travelled the world in search of exciting ideas and techniques, these two designers utilise the knowledge and experience they have gained to create unique items that are as much works of art as they are pieces of jewellery. Featuring pieces in a variety of materials, including pearl, silver, gold, coral, precious and semi-

precious stones, their philosophy is that their designs should possess an innate ageless grace that is as much an extension of the wearer's inner strength and character as it is an accessory to outer beauty. This, they feel, is more important than being trendy or trying to compete with the low-cost mass producers that tend to dominate the market at present.

To this end, they specialise in creating unique, finely crafted items, with a special emphasis paid to avant-garde pieces that have been influenced by local Croatian styles—intertwining the old with the new and the traditional with the modern. By way of illustration, one striking example of their innovative work is a letter-opener inspired by a traditional style of belt-buckle worn by the women of Dubrovnik. There are many other pieces in the same creative vein, and visitors to the 'Jewel of the Adriatic' would be well rewarded in setting aside some time to browse through its finest jewellery gallery.

FACTS

PRODUCTS	jewellery
FEATURES	one-of-a-kind pieces • traditional craft influences • natural materials
NEARBY	all attractions within Dubrovnik
CONTACT	Miha Pracata, 20000 Dubrovnik • telephone: +385.20.324 744 • facsimile: +385.51.603 509 • email: mm.design@inet.hr

PHOTOGRAPHS COURTESY OF JEWELLERY GALLERY ĐARDIN.

Nautika

Those in the know are aware that just off the main road, on the Adriatic coast beyond the Pile Gate of Dubrovnik's Old Town, is the acclaimed restaurant Nautika, a highly fêted candidate vying for the much envied title of Dubrovnik's finest dining experience.

The Nautika is a member of Croatia's acclaimed Esculap Teo restaurant group, which was started some 30 years ago, and now also includes two other equally lauded and prestigious properties: Proto, right in the bustling heart of the streets of the Old Town, and the Konavoski Dvori, perfectly located in a tranquil valley slightly east of Dubrovnik.

Nautika is set in a cove with a dramatic view of the Adriatic, eschewing showy and fanciful interiors for the classic beauty of its surroundings. A venue of such aesthetic scope is prime location for the countless culinary odysseys and televised cookery shows that have discovered this national treasure. The elegant terraces overlook a rock-strewn inlet, vistas defined by the crystalline sea and the imposing fortresses of Bokar and Lovrijenac glowing gold in the Mediterranean sun.

Aptly enough for the evocatively named Nautika, chef Nikola Ivanišević excels in the realm of seafood. His cream of scampi with black truffles is a scintillating bouquet of liquid flavour that may preface the tempting Korčula-style lobster medallions or the Lopud fish brodetto with polenta. Not that his non-seafood creations are any less exquisite. Each dish is prepared and plated to equal Nautika's magnificent marine panoramas, and diners are rarely let down. Nikola's passion lies in conveying the culinary facets of Ragusa (ancient Dubrovnik) to a new

THIS PAGE (FROM TOP): The stained glass compass which casts its coloured light over the interior; the Nautika's outdoor terrace overlooks the Adriatic, providing customers with an unparalleled sea view over a leisurely lunch.

OPPOSITE: The impressive fortresses of Bokar and Lovrijenac define the spectacular boundaries of the Nautika's panoramic views.

generation of global audiences, and guests include Pope John Paul II, film star Richard Gere, U2 front man and humanitarian Bono and Hollywood's Owen Wilson.

An alfresco lunch at Nautika is idyllic and restful, defined by the soft sea breeze from the white-capped waves below, rising through rustling foliage to cool the canopied terraces. Evening diners luxuriate in the balmy post-meridian hours against a backdrop of stars celestial in clear skies and earthbound in Dubrovnik's glittering harbour. The interior is dappled by prismatic light refracted through a stained-glass compass set into the ceiling, casting multi-hued tints over elegant furnishings, sleek wood-panelled walls and latticed windows, accentuating the Nautika's ambience and exceptional service levels.

The Nautika is the rare combination of superlative cuisine, stylish setting and service par excellence that those with a keen sense of the finer things in life cannot fail to appreciate. Its spectacular location on the Adriatic coast is merely the factor which delivers this already superb restaurant into the domain of the extraordinary, bringing it into a visit-imperative class of its own.

FACTS		
FOOD	seafood • meat dishes • contemporary & traditional Dubrovnik dishes	
FEATURES	3 interior dining rooms • 3 terraces • 2 levels	
NEARBY	Dubrovnik's Old Town • Hilton Imperial Dubrovnik	
CONTACT	Brsalje 3, 20000 Dubrovnik • telephone: +385.20.442 526 • facsimile: +385.20.442 525 • email: sales@esculap-teo.hr • website: www.esculap-teo.hr	

PHOTOGRAPHS COURTESY OF ESCULAP TEO.

Croatia Airlines

Croatia Airlines is the country's elite flagship carrier, possessing Croatia's most advanced fleet. A proud member of the Star Alliance since 2004, this national airline is helping to bring ever-increasing numbers of travellers closer to the delights of this dramatic and diverse country.

From its northern base in Zagreb, Croatia Airlines connects its passengers to Europe's thriving centres of commerce, tourism and industry, and from there on to various destinations throughout the world. Its destination list runs like a Who's Who of stylish European cities, featuring Amsterdam, Brussels, Frankfurt, London, Munich, Rome, Paris, Sarajevo, Skopje, Vienna and Zurich.

Travellers exploring the length and breadth of Croatia can avail themselves of the regular internal flights to Dubrovnik in the south, Split on the Adriatic seaboard, Zadar along the west coast and Pula in the north.

From its humble beginnings with one Cessna craft in 1989, Croatia Airlines has gone rapidly from strength to strength in scope, scale and stature. It is now one of Europe's leading mid-sized airlines, with over 15 million satisfied passengers as of 2007.

As befits a progressive fleet such as this, in-flight entertainment, catering and service levels are second to none. Alcoholic and non-alcoholic beverages as well as in-flight meals catering to those with special dietary requirements are all served with a genuine smile by reassuring, professional staff.

Croatia Airline's constantly evolving customer services programme has catalysed the many in-house improvements pushing

...the carrier of choice in Croatia.

Croatia Airlines to the forefront of air-travel in recent years. On domestic flights, children under 24 months travel for free. Mini-globetrotters and adventurers have custom meals prepared for them in child-friendly sizes and appealingly presented, so that guardians can set aside all worries about catering for their little charges.

Well underway since its implementation in 2006, Croatian Airlines' new e-ticketing system has now earned its stars, making for

a much smoother research and booking experience every single step of the way. The FlyOnline Club comes with a tiered reward system that is quickly making headway into a new generation of Internet-savvy travellers who value speed and efficiency.

Being able to collect Miles & More frequent flyer miles is another incentive to use this respected national carrier. Business Class passengers too can profit from Croatia Airlines' firm local partnerships, with great value car hire opportunities available once on land. The demographic groups of students, young people and senior citizens are equally well looked after, with a 15 per cent discount on international fares.

Croatia Airlines' friendly and helpful cabin crew are always on hand to ensure that passengers leave all cares and worries on the ground behind them. For a holiday in this beautiful Mediterranean paradise that begins within seconds of take-off, Croatia Airlines is definitely the carrier of choice.

THIS PAGE (FROM TOP): Croatia Airlines craft proudly carry the national colours of their country; the helpful and welcoming cabin crew are ever on hand to make sure each journey is a pleasure.

OPPOSITE (FROM TOP): The customer service, whether in-flight or on the ground is always excellent; Croatia Airlines, as its country's national carrier since 1989, has maintained excellent standards of travel and service throughout.

FACTS

DESTINATIONS Amsterdam • Brussels • Dubrovnik • Frankfurt • London • Lyon • Paris • Rome • Munich • Pula • Sarajevo • Skopje • Split • Vienna • Zadar • Zagreb • Zurich

IN-FLIGHT children's meals • custom diet options • promotional/tourist films • free bar

CONTACT Croatia Airlines, Savska cesta 41, 10000 Zagreb • telephone: +385.14.872 727 • facsimile: +385.16.160 152 • website: www.croatiaairlines.com

PHOTOGRAPHS COURTESY OF CROATIA AIRLINES.

Istria Itinerary

One can tell from a glance why Istria is considered Croatia's Tuscany. This peninsula, beautifully defined by the colours of green and blue, is dotted with picturesque small towns over a rolling landscape that supports a rich agricultural lifestyle. Meticulous aged stonework is typical of the architecture in this region, of an earthy, sand-coloured stone that embodies the local affinity with nature and the elements. The medieval town-fortresses of Buje, Buzet, Motovun and Groznjan are majestically resplendent in their centuries of solemn heritage, a heritage that includes a distinctive cuisine and culture of wine-making. These towns, part of so-called 'Green Istria', lie mostly in the interior of Istria, an area known for its idyllic pastoral scenes. 'Blue Istria' lies along the coastal regions, comprising long white stretches of pebble beach and far horizons of the azure Adriatic Sea. Just off the southwestern coast, the Brijuni islands are accessible through frequent ferry runs, and is a national park that hosts sporting events such as polo, and is filled with an astounding variety of flora and fauna.

Highlights:
Motovun • Buje • Buzet • Groznjan • Rovinj • Rabac • Brijuni islands

Suggested Itinerary:
- Fly into Pula with Croatia Airlines.
- Explore the beautiful coastline in the area, especially the beaches of Stoja and Verudela, reputedly the most scenic beaches in all of Istria.
- Take the ferry to the nearby Brijuni islands, a national park of reserves and open meadows that abounds in wildlife, thanks to its almost ideal microclimatic conditions. Species found in the park range from the native oxen and ornithological wildlife to imported deer, zebras, and even elephants! Veli Brijun is also a popular destination for leisure boaters, who can spend all day in the clear channels of surrounding crystalline water, enjoying the vast colonies of vivid marine life. Scuba diving is also available in guided groups, and spectacular underwater photography is often the result of such tours.
- Stop by Rovinj, coastal city with a distinctly unique town centre, with its unusual mix of historical monuments, testifying to its various cultural influences over the ages. Narrow, tall houses frame the squares, leaning one on the other, a riot of Baroque, Neoclassical and Renaissance architecture. Nearby, the island of Crveni Otok is a bather's paradise, with delightful little beach coves where visitors may spend many a pleasant afternoon.

- Move up north to Motovun, village of the giants, or so legend will have it. The tale goes that the hilltop town was built by giants, from massive stones lifted from the Mirna River valley below. Home to the longest set of stairs in Istria, the number of steps leading from the foot of Motovun hill to the pinnacle comes to a breathtaking 1,052. Those attempting to climb the entire flight will be pleased to find a lively Venetian-style town square at the top, with cafés and restaurants to quench the thirst and fortify the stomach. Overlooking the square is Hotel Kastel Motovun, a converted castle that rapidly fills up over summer when the Motovun Film Festival comes to town.

- No visit to Istria is complete without sampling its celebrated black pearls and white diamonds. These gems are none other than the black and white truffles found in the region. Zigante Restaurant in Livade-Levade near Buje specialises in truffle dishes created by a master chef.

- Explore 'Green Istria' with a farmhouse stay. Stancija Negricani, near Marcana, offers a home-like atmosphere with top levels of service and the personal touch of a hands-on hostess.

- Transfer back to Pula for flight home, or to other regions within Croatia.

adriatica.net

One of the leading tour operators in Croatia, adriatica.net is committed to the pursuit of high quality presentation, professional services and the latest technology, enabling their customers to find and book holidays according to their wishes. Their belief in an expert and personal approach to each customer as well as high quality control of services and products enables them to provide holiday opportunities that fit every travel need and preference. To book a holiday with adriatica.net or simply to find out more, call +385.1.241 5611 or visit their website at www.adriatica.net.

Dubrovnik Itinerary

"Those who seek paradise on Earth should come to Dubrovnik," the famed Irish playwright and satirist George Bernard Shaw once proclaimed, but those who wish to confirm this with their own eyes may visit the city for themselves and settle it once and for all. This ancient city that, as the Republic of Ragusa, once rivalled Venice for domination of the Adriatic in the Middle Ages is now undergoing a revival that will soon see it at the top of Europe's choicest holiday destinations. Blessed as it is with the cool days and balmy nights that characterise its Mediterranean climate and maritime location, Dubrovnik is an endless treasure box with its various charms and attractions tucked away in an intricate map of old paved streets. In the summer, cultural and artistic endeavours colour the city with vibrance as the Dubrovnik Summer Festival begins its month-long extravaganza of plays, concerts and other entertainments. National tour operator adriatica.net brings Dubrovnik out in its best light for visitors looking for an unforgettable holiday in Croatia.

Highlights:

Dubrovnik Summer Festival • Historical city walls • Orlando Column • Sponza Palace • Onofrio's fountain

Suggested Itinerary:

- Fly into Dubrovnik with Croatia Airlines.
- Transfer to Dubrovnik Old Town, a UNESCO World Heritage protected site, and spend a few days in or within walking distance of the city, the better to explore its quaint streets and alleyways. The city is a pedestrian mall, and a leisurely stroll is the best way to experience the sights and sounds to the fullest. The Pucic Palace overlooks Gundulic Square in the heart of the Old Town, while the Hilton Imperial Dubrovnik is a short walk beyond Pile Gate.
- Take a walk along the city walls. Views from the ramparts are nothing short of spectacular, encompassing a panorama of town and sea. Dubrovnik's walls are its link to the past; follow the age-worn stones and one is almost convinced of having travelled back in time. The five towers forming part of the defences are venues for various events and concerts.
- Stop into one of the city's many charming cafés or restaurants to sample a local delicacy, the sweet dish rozata, a creamy smooth custard served chilled and topped with caramel syrup.
- Come face to face with a celebrated hero from the Middle Ages, at Orlando Column. The monument was raised in the 15th century as a symbol of freedom and state independence. Orlando, widely supposed to be a direct descendant of the great Charlemagne, is a favoured meeting point of Dubrovnik residents. Follow local custom and set a date at the foot of the column before continuing together on an evening rendezvous in Dubrovnik Old Town.
- Options abound in Dubrovnik after dark. Wine bars and jazz cafés rapidly fill up with a mix of local residents and tourists, and the atmosphere is usually relaxed and friendly. The Latin nightclub Fuego is the hottest spot in town for a night filled with sizzling beats and infectious energy. Party until dawn and perk up in the morning with a steaming espresso from the cafés opening their doors on Stradun, the town's high street.
- A short boat ride away is the island of Lokrum, where a botanical garden from the time of Austrian archduke Maximilian survives. A Napoleonic fort surveys the island from on high.
- Transfer back to Dubrovnik for flight home, or to other regions within Croatia.

adriatica.net

One of the leading tour operators in Croatia, adriatica.net is committed to the pursuit of high quality presentation, professional services and the latest technology, enabling their customers to find and book holidays according to their wishes. Their belief in an expert and personal approach to each customer as well as high quality control of services and products enables them to provide holiday opportunities that fit every travel need and preference. To book a holiday with adriatica.net or simply to find out more, call +385.1.241 5611 or visit their website at www.adriatica.net.

THIS PAGE: Stradun—the main street in Dubrovnik Old Town is lined with cafés where one can sit and enjoy an evening coffee.

OPPOSITE (CLOCKWISE FROM RIGHT): The vermillion roofs of the Old Town; a hearty full breakfast is a good start to the day when preparing to explore this fascinating city; the statue of Orlando stands for the values of state independence.

index

Numbers in *italics* denote pages where pictures appear.
Numbers in **bold** denote map pages.

picturecredits

The publisher would like to thank the following for permission to reproduce their photographs:

Adam Clark/Photolibrary 97 (top)
Alan Copson/Photolibrary 41
Aldo Pavan/Grand Tour/Corbis 95 (below)
Antonio Bat/epa/Corbis 98
Atlantide Phototravel/Corbis 86
CD094 Croatia 14 (top), 17, 20 (top), 24 (below), 25 (top), 33 (below), 111 (top), 120 (top, centre and below), 122 (top), 123, 124 (top), 127 (top and below), 128 (top and below), 129, 130, 131 (top), 133 (below), 134 (top and below)
Charles Bowman/Getty Images 19
Chris Mole 25 (below)
Connie Coleman/Getty Images 53, 57, 60, 68–9

Croatian National Tourist Board 2, 5, 13, 16 (top and below), 18, 21, 22 (top and below), 23 (below), 24 (top), 28 (top and below), 29, 30, 33 (top), 34 (top and below), 36 (top), 36–7 (below), 37 (top), 38, 39 (top), 51 (top and below), 58 (top and below), 59, 61 (below), 62 (top and below), 64 (below), 65 (top), 66 (top and below), 67, 92, 93, 95 (top), 99, 108, 110, 111 (below), 112 (top), 113, 114, 115 (top), 116, 131 (below), 135
Danny Lehman/Corbis 112 (below)
Ed Kashi/Corbis 40 (top)
Eric Futran/Photolibrary 34 (centre)
Euromarine 26
Françoise Raymond Kuijper 23 (top), 40 (below), 91 (top), 115 (below), 117, 133 (top)

Gavin Hellier/Getty Images 50, 118–19
Geoff Caddick/epa/Corbis 27 (top)
Grand Tour/Corbis 88
Hans Georg Roth/Corbis 52, 90, 91 (below), 121
IFA-BILDERTEAM GMBH/Photolibrary 97 (below)
Janez Skok/Corbis 96
Jeremy Horner/Corbis 132
Jon Hicks/Corbis 56 (right), 61 (top)
Jonathan Blair/Corbis 14 (below), 122 (below)
JTB Photo/Photolibrary 42–3, 56 (left), 124–25 (below)
Keren Su/Getty Images 48
Louis-Laurent Grandadam/Getty Images 65 (below)
Marco Cauz/Corbis 20 (below)
Mark Newman/Photolibrary 39 (below)

Martin Stolworthy/Getty Images 6
Neil Emmerson/Getty Images 8–9
Nik Wheeler/Corbis 89
Owen Franken/Corbis 100–01
Panoramic Images/Getty Images 136–37
Peter Adams/Getty Images 12
Philippe Giraud/Goodlook/Corbis 35, 94
Richard I'Anson/Getty Images 4
Roland Schlager/epa/Corbis 27 (centre)
Ruggero Vanni/Corbis 54
Simeone Huber/Getty Images 126
Steve Vidler/Photolibrary 32
Thierry Orban/Corbis 27 (below)
Thomas Eckerle/Photolibrary 64 (top)
Tony Gervis/Getty Images 55
Wayne Walton/Getty Images 15, 63

directory

Adriana, hvar marina hotel and spa (page 146)
21450 Hvar
telephone : +385.21.750 750
facsimile : +385.21.750 751
email : reservations@suncanihvar.com
website : www.suncanihvar.com

Croatia Airlines (page 176)
Savska cesta 41,
10000 Zagreb
telephone : +385.14.872 727
facsimile : +385.16.160 152
website : www.croatiaairlines.com

Dubrovnik House Gallery (page 170)
Svetog Dominika 2,
20000 Dubrovnik
telephone : +385.20.322 092
facsimile : +385.20.322 091
email : ars.longa@du.t-com.hr

Euromarine (page 46)
Svetice 15,
10000 Zagreb
telephone : +385.12.325 234
facsimile : +385.12.325 237
email : charter@euromarine.hr
website : www.euromarine.hr

Hilton Imperial Dubrovnik (page 158)
Marijana Blazica 2,
20000 Dubrovnik
telephone : +385.20.320 320
facsimile : +385.20.320 220
email : sales.dubrovnik@hilton.com
website : www.dubrovnik.hilton.com

Hotel Arbiana (page 104)
Obala Petra Kresimira 12,
51280 Rab
telephone : +385.51.775 900
facsimile : +385.51.775 991
email : sales@arbianahotel.com
website : www.arbianahotel.com

Hotel Bellevue (page 160)
Pera Cingrije 7,
20000 Dubrovnik
telephone : +385.20.330 000
facsimile : +385.20.330 100
email : welcome@hotel-bellevue.hr
website : www.hotel-bellevue.hr

Hotel Dubrovnik Palace (page 162)
Masarykov put 20,
20000 Dubrovnik
telephone : +385.20.430 000
facsimile : +385.20.430 100
email : info@dubrovnikpalace.hr
website : www.dubrovnikpalace.hr

Hotel Excelsior (page 164)
Frana Supila 12,
20000 Dubrovnik
telephone : +385.20.353 353
facsimile : +385.20.353 555
email : info@hotel-excelsior.hr
website : www.hotel-excelsior.hr

Hotel Glavovic (page 156)
Obala Ivana Kuljevana,
20222 Lopud
telephone : +385.20.759 359
facsimile : +385.20.759 358
email : info@hotel-glavovic.hr
website : www.hotel-glavovic.hr

Hotel Kastel Motovun (page 74)
Trg Andrea Antico 7,
52424 Motovun
telephone : +385.52.681 607
facsimile : +385.52.681 652
email : info@hotel-kastel-motovun.hr
website : www.hotel-kastel-motovun.hr

Hotel Nautica Novigrad (page 72)
Sv Antona 15,
52466 Novigrad
telephone : +385.52.600 400
facsimile : +385.52.600 450
email : info@nauticahotels.com
website : www.nauticahotels.com

Hotel Šipan (page 154)
Šipanska Luka 160,
20223 Šipanska Luka,
Otok Šipan,
Dubrovnik
telephone : +385.20.758 000
facsimile : +385.20.758 004
email : hotel-sipan@petral.hr
website : www.hotel-sipan.com

Hotel Sv Mihovil (page 144)
Ul Bana Jelači'ca 8,
21240 Trilj
telephone : +385.21.831 790
facsimile : +385.21.831 770
email : sv.mihovil@inet.hr
website : www.svmihovil.com

Hotel Vestibul Palace (page 138)
Iza Vestibula 4,
21000 Split
telephone : +385.21.329 329
facsimile : +385.21.329 333
email : info@vestibulpalace.com
website : www.vestibulpalace.com

Hotel Villa Angelo d'Oro (page 76)
Via Svalba 38-42,
52210 Rovinj
telephone : +385.52.840 502
facsimile : +385.52.840 112
email : hotel.angelo@vip.hr
website : www.angelodoro.hr

Istravino Wines (page 106)
Tome Stri˝zi'ca 8,
51000 Rijeka
telephone : +385.51.406 670
facsimile : +385.51.406 660
email : info@istravino-rijeka.hr

Jewellery Gallery Đardin (page 172)
Miha Pracata,
20000 Dubrovnik
telephone : +385.20.324 744
facsimile : +385.51.603 509
email : mm.design@inet.hr

Le Méridien Lav Split (page 140)
Grljevacka,
Podstrana 2A,
21312 Split
telephone : +385.21.500 500
facsimile : +385.21.500 300
email : info-split@lemeridien.com
website : www.lemeridien.com/split

Nautika (page 174)
Brsalje 3,
20000 Dubrovnik
telephone : +385.20.442 526
facsimile : +385.20.442 525
email : sales@esculap-teo.hr
website : www.esculap-teo.hr

Palmizana Meneghello (page 152)
Meneghello Estate,
Palmizana,
21450 Hvar
telephone : +385.21.717 270
facsimile : +385.21.717 268
email : palmizana@palmizana.hr
website : www.palmizana.hr

The Pucic Palace (page 166)
Ulica Od Puca 1,
20000 Dubrovnik
telephone : +385.20.326 222
facsimile : +385.20.326 223
email : reservations@thepucicpalace.com
website : www.thepucicpalace.com

The Regent Esplanade (page 44)
Mihanoviceva 1,
10000 Zagreb
telephone : +385.1.456 6666
facsimile : +385.1.456 6020
email : info.zagreb@rezidorregent.com
website : www.regenthotels.com

Riva, hvar yacht harbor hotel (page 150)
21450 Hvar
telephone : +385.21.750 750
facsimile : +385.21.750 751
email : reservations@suncanihvar.com
website : www.suncanihvar.com

San Rocco Hotel + Restaurant (page 70)
Srednja Ulica 2,
52474 Brtonigla
telephone : +385.52.725 000
facsimile : +385.52.725 026
email : info@san-rocco.hr
website : www.san-rocco.hr

Stancija Negricani (page 80)
Stancija Negricani farmhouse, 52206 Marcana
telephone : +385.52.391 084
facsimile : +385.52.580 840
email : konoba-jumbo@pu.t-com.hr
website : www.stancijanegricani.com

Valsabbion (page 82)
Pjescana Uvala IX/26,
52100 Pula
telephone : +385.52.218 033
facsimile : +385.52.383 333
email : info@valsabbion.hr
website : www.valsabbion.hr

Villa Astra (page 102)
V.C. Emina 11,
51415 Lovran
telephone : +385.51.294 400
facsimile : +385.51.294 600
email : villa.astra@lovranske-vile.com
website : www.lovranske-vile.com

Villa Bale (page 78)
12 Venetian House,
47 Warrington Crescent,
London W9 1EJ
telephone : +44.845.500 2000
facsimile : +44.845.500 2001
email : info@thevillabook.com
website : www.thevillabook.com

Villa Dubrovnik (page 168)
12 Venetian House,
47 Warrington Crescent,
London W9 1EJ
telephone : +44.845.500 2000
facsimile : +44.845.500 2001
email : info@thevillabook.com
website : www.thevillabook.com

Zigante Restaurant (page 84)
Livade-Levade 7,
52427 Livade-Levade
telephone : +385.52.664 302
facsimile : +385.52.664 303
email : restaurantzigante@livadetartufi.com
website : www.zigantetartufi.com